Local Politics Matters

LOCAL POLITICS MATTERS

A Citizen's Guide to Making a Difference

Richard J. Meagher, PhD

Lantern Publishing & Media • Brooklyn, NY

2020
Lantern Publishing & Media
128 Second Place
Brooklyn, NY 11231
www.lanternpm.org

Printed in the United States of America

Library of Congress Cataloging-in-Publication Data
Name: Meagher, Richard J., author.
Title: Local politics matters : a citizen's guide to making a difference
    / Richard J. Meagher, PhD.
Description: Brooklyn : Lantern Books, 2019. | Includes
    bibliographical references.
Identifiers: LCCN 2020019912 (print) | LCCN 2020019913 (ebook)
    | ISBN 9781590566190 (paperback) | ISBN 9781590566206
    (ebook)
Subjects: LCSH: Local government—Citizen participation—United
    States. | Social action—United States. | United States—Politics
    and government.
Classification: LCC JS331 .M43 2020 (print) | LCC JS331 (ebook) |
    DDC 320.80973—dc23
LC record available at https://lccn.loc.gov/2020019912
LC ebook record available at https://lccn.loc.gov/2020019913

CONTENTS

ACKNOWLEDGMENTS

My thanks to CUNY's Alan DiGaetano and John Mollenkopf; their urban politics courses started me on a path toward this book years ago.

Thanks to Nancy Falciani-White and Seth Clabough at Randolph-Macon College for providing the space and advice to make this book a reality.

Thanks to my Honors students Anna Allen, Bridget Maas, and Melanie Wark, whose research helped inform the chapter on affordable housing.

Thanks to Heather Massa, the World's Best Children's Librarian and an even better sister, for research and ideas for the chapter on services.

Thanks to planner/activist Garet Prior, from whom I learned about both Arnstein's Ladder and Alexandria's engagement handbook.

Thanks to Christopher Gergen of Forward Cities for timely and helpful information on stadium financing and housing, on top of the usual stellar mentoring.

Thanks to my RVA Twitter fam, and anyone who has ever read, forwarded, or commented on my op-eds or blog posts. Underneath the typical social media nonsense is a smart local conversation, and I feel lucky to be part of it.

Thanks to Martin Rowe, Brian Normoyle, and the team at Lantern Publishing & Media for consistently reminding me how an editor and publisher make a book better—and excellent ones, even more so.

Thanks to my wife and two daughters, who hopefully know I love them more than I do any stadium financing deal or transit policy.

Finally, this book is dedicated to former Deputy Mayor Richard J. Meagher Sr. and former PTA President Gail Ann Meagher, whose lives demonstrate what "impact" really means.

PREFACE

LOCAL POLITICS IN A TIME OF CRISIS

When I wrote this book, the United States had not yet encountered the twin shocks of 2020: not just one national crisis, but two of them layered on top of each other. A global health emergency brought on by the COVID-19 virus has been followed by dramatic protests against racism breaking out in cities all across the country. This massive political unrest, as well as the continuing effects of the quarantine, will transform a generation of Americans. They also highlight the key point of this book: local politics matters.

What often gets lost in the endless stream of bad news about these crises is how much people rely on local governments. With unsteady leadership at the federal level, we have seen our state governors across the country step up to lead the way through the quarantine. But right behind them are mayors and county board members, along with school superintendents and principals, health district directors, and local bureaucrats. Shuttered schools and libraries are appreciated more than ever in their absence. City and county workers are picking up the trash and recycling, maintaining water and gas utilities, and putting out fires, all under challenging circumstances. I argue throughout this book that local politics impacts us just as much as national politics, if not more so. After COVID, that message should be heard more clearly.

On the other hand, the Black Lives Matter protests might demonstrate the flip side of this encouraging message: local governments are also at the center of some of our most challenging societal problems. The persistent problem of policing, particularly in minority communities, identifies a troubling lack of local leadership, with elected officials showing too much deference to local bureaucracies and especially police authority. Whereas the action in the streets has often been angry and disruptive, much of the violence we have seen has been generated by the police themselves, from beatings to the use of chemical warfare against the residents they are presumably sworn to protect. As Black Americans and their allies fight for attention to their cause, local law enforcement officers appear exactly as their opponents portray them: an occupying army.

Whether through protest or more traditional political means, therefore, more attention and engagement with local politics could not come at a better time. Under these twin crises of quarantine and unrest, city and county governments face daunting challenges:

- Local health agencies are tasked with tracking COVID cases, supporting health providers, and communicating urgent information to the public; in urban centers like New York and Miami, the number of cases almost overwhelmed local healthcare infrastructure.

- Public schools—as I note in this book, the arm of local government that often touches families the most—have been confronted with immediate obstacles for instruction, ranging from student access to technology to how to meet state and federal education standards under quarantine.

No matter how successful some districts have been in transitioning to remote learning, the lost weeks and months will have them playing catch-up for years.

- Transit agencies are threading the needle between the demands of social distancing and the need to get essential workers, including healthcare providers, to their places of employment. Bus drivers, train conductors, and ticket sellers are unexpectedly finding themselves on the frontlines of a pandemic.

- Local governments are trying to conduct regular business while implementing emergency measures under unprecedented conditions. How are local legislative bodies supposed to satisfy open records laws when they cannot even allow citizens into their chambers? How can local registrars run free and fair elections while keeping voters safely distanced from each other?

- The policing crisis reflects a number of persistent problems of local governance, including how to reform bureaucracies, allow meaningful civilian input, and eliminate the stubborn persistence of racism in our public institutions. In this book's chapter on racial equity, I note how the civil rights movement often targeted local government for reform; clearly we have not progressed as far from that moment as some might think.

Behind all of these challenges is what might be an even more formidable one: a fiscal crisis is looming. The economic damage from an economy shuttered during quarantine is already devastating to local revenue. Closed businesses cannot pay property or sales taxes. Unemployed workers cannot pay income tax to the state governments who provide essential funding to counties and municipalities. Even hospitals and healthcare systems—important employers, landowners, and political players in many localities—are left wondering how to balance emergency care for virus patients with paying the bills. The high costs of added police activity, for better or for worse, are no help, while local governments throughout the South are facing expensive relocation and removal efforts for Confederate monuments. All of these urgent challenges combine difficult choices with the question of how to pay for them.

Local governments cannot meet these challenges on their own. As I point out in this book's chapter on regional cooperation, localities generally cannot borrow money. They have to balance their budgets each year, and the COVID-19 crisis especially will make that task exceedingly difficult in the budget seasons to come. Federal leadership—and dollars—are absolutely essential in keeping local governments solvent. The feds have already started the bailout process, especially targeting small businesses, struggling industries, and taxpayers. But they cannot ignore the country's backbone of local governments; it is county and municipal officials who will continue to ensure that new businesses open up, kids are educated, parks and libraries are available, and elections run smoothly.

As has been widely observed, one of the last times the country faced a health crisis of such historic proportions was the "Spanish" flu outbreak at the end of World War I. Local governance operated in a very different environment in the early 1900s. Municipal public health agencies were barely developed; more often they not, they responded to the outbreak by feverishly downplaying it, trying to boost morale for the war effort rather than preventing spread of the disease. Chicago's public health commissioner even argued, "Worry kills more people than the epidemic." Meanwhile, citizens watched their friends and family sicken and die in numbers far exceeding the rosy picture they heard from local leaders.

Thankfully, in some ways local governments today are very, very different. First and foremost, they are doing more. As I note again and again in this book, the "increased capacity" of local governments to meet the needs of their residents will be essential in beating back the virus and recovering from its effects. Municipalities and counties already are at ground zero of economic development and employment, as well as ensuring equity and transparency in our society's response to quarantine.

Of course, in other ways, local government reform is woefully behind the times. A reckoning for local law enforcement may have finally come, with widespread debates about community policing, civilian review boards, and other new policies possibly helping to further transform local governance.

Still, despite the setbacks, we have at least learned *some* things in the century since the flu epidemic. All of the "right answers" that are in this book—the things we've learned about local governments and how vital their role is—are more relevant than ever. The quarantine's effects may slow down, but should not derail, the vital investments we need to make in transit, in local services, in regional cooperation, in affordable housing. And as the policing crisis shows us, possibly the most urgent investment we can make is in racial equity. None of these essential efforts can be sacrificed on the altar of public health or safety. In fact, they might be the best way to help our society recover from the effects of the quarantine and to answer our citizens' calls for justice: one county, city, and town at a time.

Local politics matters. Now, more than ever.

Richard Meagher
June 2020

INTRODUCTION

On April 14, 2017, over 40,000 baseball fans packed into a brand new stadium in Cobb County, Georgia, to see the Atlanta Braves in their new home. After playing in downtown Atlanta for the previous two decades, the team had engineered a move to this sprawling county just northeast of the city. The Braves beat the Padres 5–2, so fans probably left the park with a smile on their faces. Overall, though, Cobb County residents were probably not as happy.

The cost to the county's taxpayers for the new stadium, originally estimated at an already-high $276 million, had ballooned to almost $400 million. Meanwhile, residents had voted for creating new parks back in 2008, but county officials essentially diverted the funds that were meant for these parks to the stadium, and so these officials were obligated to raise additional taxes to pay for the promised parkland. The stadium was already becoming infamously hard to access particularly through public transportation, in part because of decades of the majority-white county residents' resistance to connecting to Atlanta's transportation network. Finally, voters were never given the chance to approve the stadium deal in the first place because their county commissioners refused to negotiate the deal in public; they even tried to dodge open meeting laws by literally having secret conversations in the hallways. Voters eventually threw out the county commission chair, who spearheaded the deal, although the primary election in which he was defeated featured a minuscule 10 percent turnout.

(And just in case you were wondering, the Braves finished 72–90 that year, 25 games out of first place.)

This story has a little bit of everything you can expect from local politics. It concerns development and land use—*the* issue of local governance—as well as questions of racial diversity and its effects on investments in infrastructure. Powerful interests swooped in while no one was paying attention and influenced government officials to make major decisions that would affect the financial stability and policies of their locality for decades to come. And even when taxpayers got riled up enough to take notice, hardly any of them bothered to vote.

Welcome to local politics!

These decisions facing the taxpayers of Cobb County, Georgia, are not particularly isolated or rare. Every day, all across the country, citizens are dramatically affected by decisions made in their counties, cities, towns, and by other local governments. And yet, local issues are often ignored, with only a few active participants determining issues that affect thousands. Turnout in American elections is already pretty poor by international standards, but the number of voters who participate in purely local elections is almost ridiculously small. Even people who pay attention to politics are more likely to have heard about the latest battles in Congress or a Supreme Court decision than to know who their town councilman or county supervisor is. But the decisions those local officials make often matter much more and more directly impact citizens' lives than anything that goes on in Washington.

Simply put: *local politics matters*. But hardly anyone knows it. This book is going to change that.

THINK LOCAL

When you hear about politics on television or on social media, the story probably concerns partisan squabbling in Congress or a candidate's prospects for the next Presidential election. When we take civics and government classes in high school and college (if we take them at all), the focus is likely on the national government. The model we use to teach and talk about lawmaking is most often the national legislature; the famous "I'm Just a Bill" cartoon and song from *Schoolhouse Rock* are not about municipal ordinances. If a person is knowledgeable enough to even identify the fact that government has an "executive branch," the example they would use would almost surely be the President of the United States, not their local mayor or county executive.

But it is at the local level where a lot of the action happens in American politics. Traffic laws, noise codes, and marriage licenses are all concerns of towns, counties, and cities. For example:

- If you are a homeowner or a building contractor, the permit you need to add that second bathroom comes from your local government.
- If you have kids in public schools, then the place where they spend most of their lives is governed by your local school board—which is often appointed without much public scrutiny or elected by less than 10 percent of voters.
- Even when you vote for national officials like the President or members of Congress, it is your local county or city registrar who makes sure your vote is counted.

Even state governments are more likely than the feds to handle a lot of the laws that affect you: driver's licenses are issued by states; speed limits on highways are enforced by state troopers; criminal and traffic cases are most likely handled by state or even local judges.

Of course, national government is important! Decisions made in Washington affect everyone in the United States on a host of vital issues, from healthcare to immigration to reproductive rights. But these national decisions are often implemented at the local level by state, municipal, or county officials. Think about our most debated national policy issues, from welfare to healthcare to education. Welfare offices use federal money but are run by the state. Obamacare expanded Medicaid but allowed state governments to decide whether they would do so or not. Over $500 billion in federal money goes to public schools each year, but these funds are administered by local governments and school boards.

Citizens' interest in government and politics has not been helped by the increasing partisanship and gridlock in Washington over the past few decades. Thanks largely to isolated Beltway politicians losing touch with normal Americans, faith in government has declined dramatically, with a historically low percentage of Americans—less than 20 percent in recent polls—saying they can trust the government in Washington to do what is right.

Trust in local and state government, on the other hand, is much higher, often ranging from 60 to 75 percent. Still, very few people pay attention to, let alone participate in, this level of governance. Turnout in local elections remains incredibly low, with some studies showing that only one in five voters shows up to vote even in major cities. And even those who do vote may be relatively unfamiliar with the peculiarities of local government structures. How many city residents know if they have a "strong-mayor" or "council–mayor" system of government? Does anyone know if they are subject to the decisions of a "board of supervisors"? What the heck is a "selectman"?!?

It doesn't have to be this way.

WHY SHOULD I READ THIS BOOK?

This book will make the case for local politics. Not only will I will tell you *why* you should care about your town, city, or county government, I will also tell you what you can do about it.

Political scientists have been studying local government for decades. When American political science was really getting off the ground after World War II, some of the most influential studies on democracy and politics focused on cities. And it turns out that we have learned a few things about local politics that do not rely on partisanship or ideology. You may often hear that there are always at least two sides to every political issue. But in local politics, sometimes there *are* right answers.

This book takes the knowledge that scholars have amassed from over half a century of studying local politics and translates that knowledge into clear action steps for *you, the citizen and voter.* Which candidate should you choose for mayor? If you run for city council, what should be your platform? Should you support a bond referendum? (What's a bond referendum?)

This book will do three things in particular:

1. **Explain local government.** What kinds of local governments are there? What are the differences between them? Who makes the key decisions in *my* county or town?
2. **Explain why you should care.** Local governments are doing more these days. And it is not only important to pay attention, but almost easy to get involved.
3. **Explain what to do.** There are at least six "right answers" in local governance, ranging from housing to spending to

stadium financing. When it comes to these issues, there is really only one political path that makes sense. Not only does this book lay out these six issues, it also adds specific action steps you can take—not just on these issues, but to get involved in local politics in general.

By the end of this book, you should feel informed, armed, and empowered to dive into local politics, right where you live.

THE REST OF THE BOOK

Here is what you will find in the rest of this book, chapter by chapter.

Types of Local Government

In the next chapter, I will lay out the different types of local government and introduce some of the basic vocabulary you need to know.

There are essentially two types of local government: *general-purpose* and *single-purpose*. General-purpose governments are the "regular" local governments that you normally hear about. Typically, these are either *counties* or *cities*, although there are some other designations, like "towns" or "villages," that I'll also describe.

Single-purpose governments are a little more complicated. You may be familiar with the most widespread example: school districts. We don't often think of schools as government agencies, but that is basically what they are. A school district is a local government set up with specific powers and duties to do one thing: run your local public schools. There are other, less well-known single-purpose governments as well, from water conservation districts to economic development authorities.

(Fair warning: this chapter is probably the most textbook-y part of this book. In fact, the information is based on a class I teach in state and local government. If your eyes glaze over when someone says "let's define terms," that's fine; I won't be insulted if you skip to the good stuff in the later chapters.)

Why Should I Care?

After we get those pesky definitions out of the way, I will explain the *three key reasons* why you should care about what's going on in your local city, town, or county government.

First, **local governments are doing more.** Over the past few decades, state and local governments have been asked to do more and more "stuff," from emergency management to urban bike shares to stem cell research. The fancy term for this surge is *increased capacity*: local governments now have the capacity, or ability, to do more for their citizens.

Second, **what local governments do is important.** As I have already mentioned, it may seem a little odd that so much of our political attention is aimed at Washington, DC, when so much of what affects our lives is actually decided much closer to home. Local government is most often about development and land use (where stuff gets built), but it's also about providing various kinds of services that go unnoticed—from picking up your garbage to filling potholes to providing flu shots and eye exams to impoverished kids.

Again and again, when Americans encounter a government official or they need a government service, they will most likely engage with a city or county employee or official who will provide that service to them. In fact, local government employees outnumber state employees by three to one and federal employees by almost seven to one.

Finally, **local governments are local.** There are two U.S. senators from California, a state of 40 million people. By contrast, Alpine County, the smallest county in California and located on the border of Nevada, two hours south of Reno, has about 1,200 residents; each of its five-person board of supervisors represents about 250 people. Which person—the U.S. senator or the Alpine County supervisor—is more likely to be available to hear a resident's concerns?

Alpine County may be an extreme example, but there are local governments all across the country that are not much larger. The scale of even a major city is small enough that citizens can have a big impact. What's more, local government officials are often people we know or at least they know someone we know. Their duties are often part-time, so they can maintain "real" jobs in the community. You can go and talk to these people and they should have time for you—that is if you don't see them at the grocery store or in church. Local government provides *access* in a way that national government no longer does, if it ever did. It may take thousands of letters and emails to move a national official or try to affect the federal bureaucracy, but just a handful of voices can make a huge difference at the local level.

The Right Answers

The rest of the book aims to show you what to do once you are interested in local politics.

For six selected issues, I believe that there is a right side to be on in almost all cases, so you will always know what to do the next time these issues come up in your county or city. This book will briefly explain what you need to know for each issue:

- **No taxpayer funding for a sports stadium. Ever.** We'll start with an easy one: avoid taxpayer-funded sports facilities. The example this introduction started with, the Atlanta Braves and Cobb County, is just the tip of the iceberg; we have story after story of citizens getting a raw deal when their local government gets in bed with sports teams or arena developers. It may be tough for fans to hear, but with very few exceptions, you should never, ever, *ever* let your county or city get on the hook for funding a stadium or arena.

- **Keep housing affordable.** Great localities are great for everyone, not just the rich; not-so-wealthy people need places to live, too. But you do not need public housing projects to ensure that middle-class and mixed-income housing is preserved in your city or county. This is not just the moral thing to do—although if you have a fantastic neighborhood, shouldn't everyone get a chance to live there?—but it is required for a diverse, thriving economy and culture.

- **Get on the bus.** Public transportation provides any locality with multiple benefits, from economic development to pollution reduction. You cannot fix traffic congestion by adding more roads—that only brings more cars to fill up the extra space. Instead, well-run cities and regions have well-developed bus, light rail, and commuter train lines, and you should almost always support their expansion.

- **Think regionally.** Local governments essentially act like lone wolves in the winter because, in some sense, they are all fighting for the same scarce scraps of food. I will explain how the structure of our politics ends up putting localities in competition with each other and how regional cooperation efforts can produce better outcomes for all involved. Getting cities and counties to work together is difficult but almost always worth it.

- **Don't cut spending (too much).** Of course, everyone should want their government to use funds as efficiently as possible. But if you support tax cuts just for the sake of cutting spending and do not pay attention to how much local government might be gutted as a result, you could end up living in a place you do not like very much. Smart leaders know that cities and localities need services: parks, schools, libraries, and even programs for the poor are part of what makes your neighborhood a great place to live in.

- **Diversity matters.** There is one rule you should probably keep in mind at any level of American politics: *Race. Always. Matters.* As much as we try to pretend otherwise, there is a long history of racism in local governance that still affects how cities and counties operate. Although there has been better news lately, local governments are often on the frontline of attempts to overcome racial disparities. A majority-black city does not require a black mayor, but it helps when representatives in local government reflect the demographics of their constituents. Diversity in government leads to everyone having a voice and to better outcomes for all.

To help the reader along, every one of these chapters concludes with a short summary, key takeaways, and a bibliography for further reading. (Of course, the reading is optional, in case you are afraid of homework.) These issues are not exactly simple, but they are easier to figure out than, say, what to do about climate change or the Second Amendment of the U.S. Constitution. After you read these chapters, you should have a pretty good idea of what to do the next time someone in your city or county proposes a new bus line, housing tax credit, or stadium development plan.

What to Do Next

In the last chapter of this book, I will compile all the action steps from the rest of the book into one easy list. I will also detail the three "big picture" actions you can and should do next to get started in local politics:

- **Vote.** This may seem obvious! But local elections are sometimes held in odd years, at odd times. You will probably notice when the next Presidential election season arrives even if you do not pay that much attention to politics, but you may miss hearing about that off-year school board election or April bond referendum. Voting is important for any democratic government to work properly, but your vote simply counts more at the local level because the scale and scope of the election are so much smaller. Your vote in a local election can really make a huge difference.

- **Join up.** One individual's voice and vote can matter most at the local level. But one other rule of national politics also applies here: your voice counts even more if you can combine it with others. Politicians at any level like to be responsive to their constituents and also efficient with their time: if a group of their constituents speaks with one voice, they usually listen. And whereas you can join your local chapter of the NRA or ACLU, there is another kind of interest group that matters even more in local politics: the *neighborhood civic association*. These local neighborhood groups—or substitutes like neighborhood watches, homeowners associations, or even informal group meetings—can provide a structure for public officials to meet with residents and hear their concerns. You should join one of these groups; if none exists, you should start one.

- **Go to a public meeting.** Almost every city council, town board, or county commission meets at least monthly, if not weekly, and their meetings, by law, are open to the public. Local governments are often subject to rules that make sure they solicit public input on policymaking, often at these meetings, although more and more they also receive comments online and through other means. Still, no matter how they get input, you can be the voice they hear! Not only can you attend meetings and make your voice heard, you can also make sure officials listen better. There are rules and guidelines for running open, accessible governments, and you can work to help make sure your local government implements those guidelines.

You cannot win every political fight. But at the local level, at least, you *can* make yourself heard. Armed with the knowledge in this book—and hopefully even a little inspired by it—you can become a powerful political voice in your own town, city, or county.

So get reading, and then get out there!

SUMMARY

- When (or if) they think about politics, most people think at the national level. But <u>local politics</u> may affect our lives even more directly.
- This book <u>explains local government</u>, tells you <u>why you should care</u>, and tells you <u>what you can do</u> about it.
- The book also contains six <u>right answers</u>; unlike at the national level, there are some issues at the local level where there really is just one course of action that makes sense.
- The book also has some general <u>action steps—voting</u>, joining a <u>neighborhood group</u>, and attending a <u>public meeting</u>—that will help you make a difference in your city or county.

ACTION STEPS

- *Read the rest of the book!*

WANT TO KNOW MORE?

If you want to learn more about the gory details of the Cobb County stadium deal, you could start by reading coverage from the essential *Field of Schemes* website (more on that in the stadium chapter below); the website's main author, journalist Neil deMause, also provided a nice overview of the Braves story for *Vice* in 2016.

Polling data on trust in government can come from a number of sources. The Gallup organization has been asking questions about this issue for decades and has noted the high levels of trust in local government on their website and in a number of reports. Similarly, there is a lot of data on low voter turnout in local elections. The most authoritative academic source is a 2013 journal article in *Political Science Quarterly* by political scientists Thomas M. Holbrook and Aaron C. Weinschenk, although Portland State researchers also have quality work featured on their more user-friendly website, www.whovotesformayor.org.

BIBLIOGRAPHY/FURTHER READING

Brown, T. M. 2017. "The Braves' New Ballpark Is an Urban Planner's Nightmare." *Deadspin*. August 10. https://deadspin.com/the-braves-new-ballpark-is-an-urban-planners-nightmare-1797593063.

deMause, Neil. 2016a. "Tim Lee Steamed at Reports He Siphoned off Parks Money for Braves Stadium (But Yeah, He Sure Did)." *Field of Schemes*. June 8. http://www.fieldofschemes.com/2016/06/08/11197/tim-lee-steamed-at-reports-he-siphoned-off-parks-money-for-braves-stadium-but-yeah-he-sure-did/.

———. 2016b. "Cobb County and the Braves: Worst Sports Stadium Deal Ever?" *Vice*. June 9. https://www.vice.com/en_us/article/qkyk3v/cobb-county-and-the-braves-worst-sports-stadium-deal-ever.

Holbrook, Thomas M., and Aaron C. Weinschenk. 2014. "Campaigns, Mobilization, and Turnout in Mayoral Elections." *Political Research Quarterly* 67 (1): 42–55. https://doi.org/10.1177/1065912913494018.

McCarthy, Justin. 2018. "Americans Still More Trusting of Local Than State Government." *Gallup.com*. October 8. https://news.gallup.com/poll/243563/americans-trusting-local-state-government.aspx.

LOCAL GOVERNMENT

THE BASICS

It's time to get some academic, textbook-type stuff out of the way. I know this feels like *learning* (ugh). But it helps to know some basic vocabulary and just a little bit about the varieties of local government. This chapter will give you three key bits of information:

- **Types of local government**: it may seem obvious, but there are plenty of different local governments aside from your basic cities and counties; there are also towns and villages, plus specialized government bodies that cover anything from airports to zoos.
- **Structure**: different local governments have different names for their elected and appointed officials, from "council member" to "supervisor" to "selectman." How are these people organized? Who has what kind of powers?
- **Vocabulary**: if you go to a local government meeting, you might hear a lot of terms that you did not hear even in a high school or college government class. What's an

"assessor"? What's the difference between a "proclamation" and a "resolution"? What's an "ordinance"? (It's not military firepower.)

By the end of this chapter, you will have a better sense of how local government works and its scope. Then you can be better prepared to go get involved.

WHAT IS A LOCAL GOVERNMENT?

Charters

The first thing to understand about local governments is that they exist solely as creations of their state governments. More specifically, they are "chartered" by states to help implement state policies and to govern at the local level. This means that in most cases, the state government has literally issued a charter or document to your local county or town to give it legal standing as a "real" place.

For many states, especially the older ones on the East Coast, this means that state laws and constitutions often authorized only localities that already had existing borders. Even a relative newcomer like Nevada, formed in 1864, has very little language in its constitution about counties. Counties were already facts of life in the territory before statehood, so the document just says that "The Legislature shall establish a system of County and Township Government which shall be uniform throughout the State."

Because states authorize local governments, that means that if a state decides to eliminate a local government, it can; technically, your city can "disappear" through a state legislative action. In reality, this almost never happens unless a locality wants it. In the early 2000s in Virginia, for example, a couple of cities wanted to give up their separate status and become absorbed into adjacent counties. So the state passed laws that basically revoked their charter, turning them into towns. This all sounds magical, but it obviously does not have any effect on the land, buildings, homes, or residents; everyone just ends up living under a different local government. This "magic" works in reverse with newly created localities as well: also in the early 2000s, Sandy Springs broke off from the city of Atlanta and became its own Georgia locality—without anyone having to move their house an inch.

Since they are beholden to state authority, local governments have significant limits to their power. For instance, activists in southern cities have often argued for the removal of Confederate monuments from their local streets. Defenders of such monuments say they do not want to erase history, but their opponents counter by pointing out how most local monuments were erected during segregation as symbols of white power. I do not want to get too far into that debate here, but I bring it up to make this point: it is largely irrelevant. Most cities have little to no power to remove any monument to Robert E. Lee or Stonewall Jackson. Sometimes this is because the monument might be on state land, or maybe it is privately owned—or maybe it's the fault of a dead guy named Dillon.

Huh?

Some states are called "Dillon's Rule" or just "Dillon Rule" states, after an Iowa judge named John F. Dillon. Back in 1868, Judge Dillon issued a couple of rulings that codified the idea that local governments can *only* do the things they are *expressly allowed* to do by state government in either laws or the state constitution. According to Dillon—and since it upheld his rulings against challenges decades later, the U.S. Supreme Court—local governments cannot do anything new without first getting permission from their state governments. If citizens in the city of Charlotte want to take down a monument, that's the call of the North Carolina state legislature, not Charlotte's city government.

In general, good government types see the Dillon Rule as too restrictive, especially in an era of increased capacity where local governments are asked to take a more active role in policymaking.

And there are plenty of examples of these restrictions preventing local governments from accomplishing routine actions because of fears that they are overstepping their power. One probable example of peak Dillon Rule madness happened in Virginia in 2011, when Chesterfield County asked the state legislature to pass a law just to allow them to let a retiring longtime firefighter keep his fire helmet!

As a result of examples like this, most states have implemented various "home rule" provisions that loosen Dillon restrictions and empower local governments. Still, many of the home rule provisions still require "enabling" legislation from the state legislature or they apply only to specific types or sizes of government. Inertia is strong in politics, and state legislators are busy; plus, they may be reluctant to give up power when they can use that power to affect issues in their home districts. Overall, there is welcome momentum toward home rule across the country, but progress is slow.

TYPES OF LOCAL GOVERNMENT

There are two principal types of local government—**general-purpose**, and **single-purpose** (see Figure 1). Let's start with general-purpose governments first—these are your basic local governments and are only called "general" to distinguish them from single-purpose governments (which we'll get to).

Types of Local Government

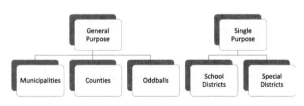

Figure 1

General-Purpose Local Governments

General-purpose local governments do the basic stuff that any government does: collect taxes; provide services like parks, libraries, and health clinics; handle law enforcement, infrastructure and roads; and so on. Everyone in the U.S. lives under the jurisdiction of at least one of these general-purpose authorities. These governments mostly fall into one of two categories—counties or municipalities—although we will talk about a third, grab-bag category of "oddballs."

Counties

Every state is completely subdivided into counties, although in Louisiana they are called parishes and in Alaska, boroughs. (Louisiana's naming convention goes back to the Roman Catholic influence on the colony under early French and Spanish rule. Alaska . . . well, it just gets mighty cold in Alaska.) For every state but two—Connecticut and Rhode Island, for various historical reasons—counties are important local governments. There are over 3,000 county governments in the U.S., and they remain a persistent fact of American political life. While other governments have changed in number and emphasis over time, states rarely rework county borders. They basically are what they are, and they are very unlikely to change.

The stability of the county government structure goes back a long way—in coastal states, back to precolonial times. Counties arose roughly out of pre-existing, unofficial borders to become the defining boundaries of many local communities. Then and now, the county's main purpose is to implement state policies at the local level. Especially back when travel was difficult and most people stayed close to home, the county "seat"—typically just a local courthouse—was the local arm of the state government. If a member of the community had any experience with local government at all, it was probably there.

This local experience was, and remains, especially true for the legal system. State courts, prosecutors, judges, and jails do a lot of the work when it comes to criminal justice, civil trials, family disputes and social service issues, and small claims and traffic enforcement; and most of this system operates at the county level. Some of these state court systems are more complicated than others—an organizational chart of the New York state court system might make your eyes water—but most states organize this work through county-level "circuit" or "district" courts, county jails, and county-level state attorneys. Local county courthouses, therefore, are where most of American justice happens.

But as the story of increased capacity would suggest, county governments do much, much more than just what happens in the courts, especially today. The typical county offers a variety of services, programs, and regulations that require experts and support staff, extensive county legal and regulatory codes, and funding. These services can include:

- Police, fire, and EMS departments
- Parks and recreation departments that manage county parks and offer youth summer camps and sports programs
- Building inspectors who issue home and commercial permits for construction
- Public libraries
- Health and social service departments that offer health clinics, substance abuse treatment and referrals, and mental health support
- Registrar offices that run *all* elections, from local to presidential

Counties are doing more because people want more from their governments. Of course, this leads to complaints, particularly from local homeowners and businesses, about costs. Because most local governments are funded chiefly by property taxes—again, local politics is often about land use—doing more "stuff" necessitates more of this tax revenue to pay for it. (We'll talk more about this when we get to schools.)

Municipalities

A municipality is the other main type of general-purpose government. Most municipalities are cities, and the terms are often used interchangeably. It may be obvious, but cities have a long history extending back to ancient civilizations; the first "nations" were really city-states, like Athens or Sparta. In the U.S., the city as a government body basically arose alongside the county structure to acknowledge growing population centers. In most American states, almost everyone lives in a county, but only concentrations of people become cities or municipalities.

While these municipal structures can be called by different names, the legal basis for their existence comes from the idea of *incorporation*, where the state issues some kind of charter or recognition of the community's legal borders. Again, "city" is the term most often used for this kind of structure. However, some states also incorporate towns, townships, or villages, either alongside the city or in place of it; the state of New York, for example, has cities, towns, *and* villages. There are over 35,000 incorporated local governments in the U.S. that are not counties, with only half of them officially being called cities. Most cities and municipalities exist within county borders, although a few cities (mostly in Virginia) are considered "independent"—they operate basically as parallel to counties. Most Americans live in or near municipalities of one kind or another.

Cities, as population centers, have many challenges. The largest cities are often regional centers of culture, power, and wealth; they also contain concentrations of poverty, segregation, and other social problems that burden their governments. For decades, cities have been the center of racial disparities, discrimination, and tension (as we'll talk about in a later chapter). All municipalities also have the same problem that faces any local government: how to use land and other resources to provide services for their residents. Although most people live in urban areas, the country overall has lacked any kind of focus on municipal or local government since the 1960s, when the federal government last had an "urban policy."

Oddballs

Municipalities and counties cover most general-purpose local governments. Still, there are a few oddballs out there that you may want to know about.

I noted above that *towns* and *townships* are one kind of municipality. But some folks see towns as something particularly different from other kinds of incorporated communities. The whole state of Indiana is divided into townships that are quite separate from county borders. In some areas, the idea of a town conveys something more rural and/or smaller than an urban population center. You can see this reflected in parts of New England, where the "town meeting" tradition of direct democracy still thrives. In Massachusetts, for example, towns with fewer than 6,000 residents are required to hold open town meetings every year, in which every town resident can vote on the budget and other matters of import.

To outsiders, New York City may be just another municipality, but it is such a unique and enormous one that it has its own type of local government. The city includes within its borders five counties; at some point, the state created *boroughs* (*not* the same as the Alaska version of counties) to help the city manage its constituent parts. So Queens is a borough of New York City although it has the same boundaries as Queens County. Each borough has a president and borough board, although their powers have been largely advisory since the late 1980s.

Whereas cities and counties generally developed along parallel paths, some communities have found it useful to merge them. The most prominent example of a *consolidated city–county* government is probably Philadelphia: Philly is obviously a city, but it also functions as a county, with the same powers as other counties within the state of Pennsylvania. A city and county both exist nominally within such places (unlike independent cities), but they are essentially the same entity with two different names, with the city operating all county functions.

Thanks to the country's shameful history of its treatment of Native Americans, the federal government has designated or "reserved" specific lands for sovereign Native American tribes and nations. *Reservations* are, therefore, local governments that are directly recognized by the federal government. Often but not always run by tribal councils, these general-purpose governments may have tribal courts and their own law enforcement. In other ways, though, reservations completely bypass local and state governments and operate like independent lands under federal jurisdiction; the FBI, rather than local or state police, is responsible for handling major crimes on reservations. Thanks to a variety of federal and state regulations, and thanks to a mishmash of land use rules—land may be publicly, privately, or tribally owned—these local governments are probably the least like any other.

There are plenty of other oddball categories out there, including *territories*, like Puerto Rico, with their own local government structures; *Washington, DC*, a federally created municipality that exists outside of the state–county–city structure in unique ways; *unincorporated areas*, a term of art for vaguely defined communities without any official government structure; and probably others. All of these oddballs should remind us that local government arose from centuries of varied practices and shifting historical boundaries. In a federalist system like ours, where each state has its own unique rules and culture, nothing is truly uniform, least of all local government.

Single-Purpose Local Governments

The principle of single-purpose government should not be too hard to grasp—the term refers to a local government structure devoted to one function only. The most obvious example is the type of government that people probably interface with the most out of all types and levels: school districts, which run K–12 public education. Still, there are plenty of other examples of "special" governments designed for a variety of functions, and their use is only growing.

School Districts

We do not always think of public schools as government agencies, but that is exactly what they are. Teachers are not just public employees, but bureaucrats who implement government policy. (That is not meant as an insult.) School boards are governing bodies, often set up to "rule" the city or county, just for the one specific purpose of running their community's school system.

On the East Coast, borders of a school district typically coincide with those of a similar general-purpose government; for example, counties often have county-wide school systems. In the West and Midwest, the districts more often have no relation to other local government borders. As with general-purpose governments, how districts operate ranges from state to state. California has over a thousand school districts, some of which run only specific levels of schools—a high school district vs. an elementary school district, for example. On the other hand, Hawaii operates just one single school district, with a statewide board of education overseeing all public schools in the state.

There used to be many more school districts than there are today. Local schools started as community-funded endeavors, but were eventually organized into systems and professionalized. More and more, local governments are moving toward consolidation of school functions into larger districts, probably in an effort to reduce costs. Census data shows that over the last half-century, the country went from almost 70,000 school districts to fewer than 13,000.

Most school boards are elected bodies, sometimes chosen in off-year or spring elections. The idea of these unconventional elections is to make them less "political" by separating them from their more partisan cousins in November—although board candidates are often partisan figures and go on to careers in "regular" politics, particularly in cities. Some states allow for yes/no votes on the budget as well, either under special circumstances—a bond issue (often called a "bond referendum") to borrow money to build, say, a new school—or as part of an annual approval process.

In general, there is a debate about whether any of this is a good idea—budget referenda, off-schedule elections, or even whether school board members should be elected or appointed. It reflects a general tension in democracy between accountability and expertise. (We often hear the same debate about elections for judges as well.) You want officials to be accountable, but do voters know enough about school administration to know who the best candidate might be or how money should be spent?

Financing is a prominent issue, if not the key issue, for school districts. Most school systems are financed through a combination of federal grants to states, direct state funding, and local property taxes. Most states try to allocate their state and federal funds using an "equalization formula" in order to make up for the gap in property tax revenue between rich and poor districts. School district costs are often reduced to a line item in the budget of their "parent" government—the overlapping or nearby municipality or county. This often leads to tension between the "parent" government and taxpayers: the argument basically boils down to "Give us more money!" vs. "You don't spend it well!"

Special Districts

A growing trend in local government is to create other single-purpose governments to meet a host of different demands. And there are many ways in which a community may have needs that cannot be addressed well by a single-purpose local government. For example, a problem may extend beyond a local government's borders, like a river that floods over three different counties. Or there may be a technical need that a city or county feels would be better served by an expert governing body, like providing electric service or promoting economic development. Or sometimes state and local regulations require specialized expertise and focus: for instance, many states have established soil and water conservation districts due to federal requirements to prevent flooding. Thanks to all of these needs, the number of special districts has more than tripled over the past fifty years to almost 40,000.

There are at least two ways to think about these specialized government bodies. You can consider them geographically based entities that have a job to do in a specific area, like a school district. Single-purpose governments usually involve the creation of a juris-diction that is, like a school district, coterminous with either an existing county or city, or multiple overlapping ones. Or you can think about these government bodies functionally, in the sense that they are created for a specific *purpose*—like running an airport, jail, or hospital. In fact, many special governments are referred to as "authorities" rather than "districts" because the area they cover is less important than the thing they do.

These districts or authorities can grow to become powerful regional bodies. The Port Authority of New York/New Jersey is in charge of ports, bridges and tunnels, and other transportation hubs in and around New York City; its budget is in the billions. However, special districts can also be tiny, local boards focused on obscure purposes. The City of Chesapeake, Virginia, operates a Mosquito Control Commission with a board of mostly volunteers. Still, even this minor function requires an annual budget of over $4 million, funded by specifically directed property taxes in the area.

Again, the chief concern with special districts is democratic accountability. Because they are so specialized, the operations of these governments are often overlooked by citizens; and because they are most often run by appointed boards, they are insulated from democratic control. This lack of accountability can lead them to operate in ways that might be wasteful or even irresponsible. A 2018 report from the Illinois Policy Institute, for example, notes how local park districts in the state spent over $1.5 million on promotional materials alone. (That's a lot of park brochures.)

LOCAL GOVERNMENT STRUCTURE

There are many ways in which local government bodies can be organized. Still, most local governments fall into one of a few types.

Almost all general-purpose local governments have some form of **mayor–council government**, even if the terms they use are different. (Since counties do not typically have a "mayor," a better term may be an **executive–council government**.) This model follows the old idea of the two "active" branches of government being the legislative branch, which makes the laws, and the executive branch, which administers or enforces them. So the mayor–council form makes sure that some kind of board or council passes laws that are then administered in some way by an executive branch.

Local Government Structures:
Executive-Council with "Weak" Executive

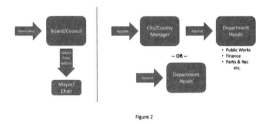

Figure 2

One version of this mayor–council government involves a
"**weak-mayor**" or executive system (see Figure 2). This "weak"
label has nothing to do with the power of the individual executive leader (or how much weight on a barbell they can deadlift).
Rather than being a separate executive, the "weak" mayor is typically selected by the council itself, from within its ranks. As a
result, this person mostly runs council meetings and holds some
ceremonial power for ribbon-cutting and the like. In this model,
the council basically operates as a legislature *and* an executive, both
passing laws and being in charge of the day-to-day operations of
the government, especially through appointment of key department heads like the head of public works or the police chief.

Local Government Structures:
Executive-Council with "Strong" Executive

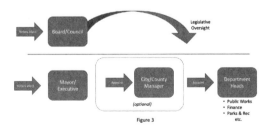

Figure 3

By contrast, a "**strong-mayor**" system (see Figure 3) has an executive who is elected separately from the council and who holds distinct executive power. This mayor or executive is typically able to directly appoint the heads of the executive branch departments.

Either one of these types of governments—strong or weak—may be combined with a **council–manager** form of government. Here, whoever is in charge of the executive branch, whether it's a separately elected executive or the elected council, would appoint a manager to run government operations. Even strong-mayor systems, where you already have one person technically in charge of the executive branch, have found it useful to have in place a chief administrator of some kind.

The governments of cities and other municipalities are often differentiated by size, with larger cities tending to favor strong-mayor structures. The more you ask a government to do, the more likely it is that citizens will see a strong executive as necessary. (Back in the day Alexander Hamilton made the same arguments in our Constitution for the presidency.) Counties are more likely to follow a weak-mayor system, although some counties do feature separately elected executives.

The names for all of these offices vary dramatically by locality. Most cities feature a city "council" and of course, a mayor. But counties that follow the strong-mayor system may have a county executive, a mayor, or even a "county judge." County legislative branches show even more variation, especially by state, with names like:

- County Council (South Carolina)
- County Commission or Board of County Commissioners (Pennsylvania)
- Board of Supervisors (Virginia)
- Board of Chosen Freeholders (New Jersey)
- Commissioners Court (Texas)

Some states even feature more than one name: in Pennsylvania, Bucks County has commissioners while Allegheny County has a council.

As for single-purpose governments, school boards almost always operate using the weak-mayor form. The school board is the council, with a board president selected from within like a weak mayor; the board selects a manager—in this case, a superintendent—to handle day-to-day operations. Most other single-purpose governments are appointed, either by councils, mayors, state officials, or some combination of these; the handful of bodies that have taxing authority are more likely to be elected. Almost all of these special districts operate like a weak-mayor council, electing a chair from among themselves.

As always with local governments, there are plenty of exceptions. For example, some localities operate a government by **commission**, where voters elect representatives who essentially serve as the head of a particular government department. So, in Portland, Oregon, the only major city that still operates this way, commissioners are elected to at-large positions, then assigned to specific departments by the mayor. According to the National League of Cities, less than 1 percent of municipalities still retain this form of government, and most observers see it as outdated.

Some New England governments include a **board of selectmen**, a tradition connected to the town meeting form of government that persists in many communities there. Historically, the town would literally identify a few "select men" to run the town meeting. Currently, the term can refer to municipal council members, town meeting conveners, or electoral officials, and practice varies by state and even locality.

LOCAL GOVERNMENT VOCABULARY

There are a few other local government vocabulary words you should probably know:

- **Ordinance**: a law passed by a municipality or county.
- **Code**: the individual laws that are passed by a city or county are typically compiled into a "code of ordinances." In recent years, the city or county code is likely to be housed in an online database—which makes it a lot easier to find out when and if your lazy neighbor can be forced to cut their grass.
- **Resolution**: as with the national government, local governments can issue a statement of opinion. Resolutions typically do not have the force of law but let a council or board offer their collective thoughts on a policy issue, national controversy, or local matter. When similar statements are issued by a mayor or other executive branch official, they are typically called **proclamations**.
- **Zoning**: many local laws and regulations concern what can be built where. (Again, local politics is all about land use.) Laws often specifically designate an area or "zone" as commercial or residential, or limit the size and scope of any development. Elected councils have the final say on any change or exception to these rules, but they often follow the recommendation of appointed **zoning boards** on all but the most controversial matters, so these boards— which may be considered single-purpose governments, depending on their structure—can have a powerful influence on local development.

Finally, there are several notable officials in different local governments, ranging from financial officers to auditors to a variety of administrators. Some of the most prominent ones include:

- **Clerk**: the chief administrator for a local government. "Clerk" is a generic term for the person who knows how to use the computer and find the files, but a city or county clerk can often be an appointed or even elected official who is responsible for a range of public functions, from maintaining the code of ordinances to issuing marriage licenses.

- **Registrar**: the official—and office—responsible for administering elections. These local workers are the backbone of the American body politic. Most of them are incredibly dedicated, competent, and fiercely independent; in the rare cases that they are not any of these, however, the danger to democracy cannot be understated.

- **Sheriff**: a law enforcement officer, often elected, with a variety of responsibilities and functions. In some states, like California, a sheriff acts as the chief of a county's police force. In other states, like Virginia, the sheriff mostly administers a locality's jails.

- **Treasurer**: this officer, either elected or appointed and sometimes called by the more accurate name of "Tax Collector," typically issues tax bills and ensures local taxes are filed and paid each year.

- **Assessor**: since most localities are funded largely by property taxes, the assessment office has an important role—determining the value of property within city or county limits.

- **Auditor, Inspector General**: different localities may have either or both of these offices, or may combine their duties into one office. In general, auditors review the finances of city and county departments to ensure that money is being properly spent, while IG offices look for fraud and criminal activity.

As noted, many of these positions are elected, again raising the question of how to balance expertise and accountability. Democratic control is terrific in theory, but localities are often criticized for a "long ballot" with too many positions, about which voters are completely uninformed. For most good government advocates, specific functions like finance and administration are often better served by appointed officials than by ambitious politicians. This can be especially true for local judges, many of whom are elected to their position: impartiality and independence might be more important than democratic accountability in the just administration of the law.

SUMMARY

- Local governments are creations of state governments; Dillon's Rule limits local authority, although states are loosening these restrictions through home rule.
- Most local governments are either general-purpose ("regular" governments) or specialized single-purpose governments.
- General-purpose governments include municipalities/ cities, counties, and some oddballs like towns, boroughs, and reservations. Single-purpose governments have specific functions, the chief example being school districts.
- Local governments can be structured in different ways, with most using a mayor–council form of government. Most counties and smaller cities use a "weak-mayor" system, with an executive chosen from the council; larger cities have a separately elected "strong" mayor. More and more localities are combining these with a council–manager government, with an appointed administrator who runs day-to-day operations.
- It helps to know some key terms like ordinances (local laws) or zoning (laws/regulations that determine what you can build where).

ACTION STEPS

- *Advocate for home rule in your state; in general, the more local control, the better.*
- *Find out which form (for example, "weak-mayor") your local government uses, and try to learn some of the lingo/vocabulary so you are better informed.*

WANT TO KNOW MORE?

You can find most of the information above and much more in a good state and local government textbook; I am partial to Bowman and Kearney's *State and Local Government.*

It is difficult to find an "official" list of Dillon Rule states. A 2010 report from the National Association of Counties, titled *County Authority*, does a thorough job of explaining the state of home rule at that time and is available on its Nevada affiliate's website at http://www.nvnaco.org/wp-content/uploads/County-Authority-a-State-by-State-Report.pdf. As much as I steer students away from this type of resource, Wikipedia's page on home rule (https://en.wikipedia.org/wiki/Home_rule_in_the_United_States) is actually updated pretty often, so that is also not a bad place to start. Still, it is probably best to check with your state's constitution to verify any home rule provisions.

Again, while any solid textbook will do, the National League of Cities (NLC) has a nice primer on different types of local government at https://www.nlc.org/forms-of-municipal-government.

Alongside the NLC, there are different national associations for many types of local government. You can read and learn about the National Association of Counties at https://www.naco.org and the National Association of Towns and Townships at http://www.natat.org. (Here's another reason why towns may be different from other municipalities: at least they see themselves as different enough to have their own associations.)

Some state governments maintain lists of special districts, but the maze of local government is not always well documented. (In general, Google is your best option.) On the other hand, localities often maintain updated lists of local boards and commissions, some of which are special districts. Your local government website may even list vacancies and offer volunteer/appointment applications.

BIBLIOGRAPHY/FURTHER READING

Bowman, Ann O'M., and Richard C. Kearney. 2017. *State and Local Government*. 10th ed. Boston: Cengage.

Illinois Policy Institute. 2018. "Waste Watch: Nearly $100M of Waste in Illinois State and Local Government." Chicago: Illinois Policy Institute.

Sellers, Matthew. 2010. "County Authority: A State by State Report." Washington, DC: National Association of Counties.

WHY SHOULD I CARE ABOUT
LOCAL POLITICS?

When Americans think about politics—if they think about politics at all—they usually focus on the national level. Who is the latest senator to announce they may be running for president? Did the Supreme Court release a new decision? Who will win in the latest showdown in Congress between the Democrats and Republicans? Once you add in international politics, with dramatic concerns about humanitarian issues and global warfare, it may seem difficult to get excited about a local zoning board meeting.

It does not help that the real nuts and bolts of governing are often kind of boring. There is a reason why CNN chyrons, newspaper headlines, and social media clickbait links are all about "battles" and "showdowns," or "crisis" and "scandal": even national politics can seem dry without these dramatic storytelling effects laid on top. But it seems like local government is doubly disadvantaged: even when there are more exciting things going on in your city or county than you might think, everyone's attention is focused on Washington instead of around the corner.

And yet, local government does so much that directly affects your life and the lives of everyone around you! Your schools, property tax rates, garbage pickup in your neighborhood, the nearest library, homeless shelter, and fire station—all of these are handled by your local government.

In this chapter, I lay out the *three key reasons* why you should care about what is going on in your local city, town, or county government:

1. Local governments are **doing more**.
2. Local government policies and actions are **increasingly important** to the daily lives of you and those around you.
3. Local governments offer **access**—you can actually talk to local government officials—and **impact**—you can make a difference.

I'll explain each one of these reasons below.

LOCAL GOVERNMENTS ARE DOING MORE

Over the past few decades, state and local governments have been asked to do more and more "stuff." They have responded with new laws and regulations, an expanded scope of action, and increased activity in all branches of government. As noted above, the fancy term for this, according to political scientists (and my favorite local politics textbook authors) Ann O'M. Bowman and Richard C. Kearney, is **increased capacity**. Local governments have developed more and more capacity, or ability, to respond to the needs of their citizens.

Numerous trends in local government have created demand for this increased capacity. Modern governments are expected to be efficiently and expertly run. This is especially true in the South, where the expansion of civil rights has led governments to have to work harder to serve all residents rather than just white ones. (Atlanta, Georgia, or Birmingham, Alabama, simply had to get bigger when their governments stopped ignoring black citizens' needs—see the chapter on race below.) At the same time, trends in national government, including sporadic Republican efforts at "devolution"—dismantling federal bureaucracies and returning power to the state and local level—have empowered localities in areas like welfare policy and healthcare delivery. And when the national mood has outpaced federal action on an issue, state and local governments have been more responsive to public opinion; for instance, the city of Ann Arbor, Michigan, decriminalized the possession of marijuana as far back as 1972.

This increased capacity is in part not just about demand from citizens, though, but the other side of the "supply and demand" equation, as local governments have been able to develop the tools to supply more services. Local clerks, officials, and judges are better trained for and more informed about best practices than they have ever been. The modernization of government has accelerated in the last decade thanks to better communication and technology. Being able to pay your parking ticket online may not be the most exciting thing ever, but it is an enormous step forward in government efficiency, and thanks to social media, local parks and public works departments can get the word out on recreation programs and road construction more widely and easily than ever. Governments use new technology to reach more citizens, perform tasks more efficiently, raise more revenue through taxes and fees, and do more in general—efficiently and competently.

As a result of this expanded activity, cities, counties, and states are communicating with one another and working together more often. Municipal leagues and counties have lobbyists in state governments; some try to petition and work with the national government as well. "Policy diffusion" is another fancy name political scientists use to describe the process of state and local laws spreading across regions or the entire country. Through this process, new laws establishing casinos, legalizing drugs, and banning smoking have been adopted by more and more localities as they see the effects of these laws outside their borders.

Still, increased capacity also brings challenges. Localities find themselves at odds with each other over issues such as natural resources and economic development (although as we'll see in a later chapter, economics has always been a point of conflict for local governments). They also find themselves in conflict with state governments over Dillon Rule restrictions and even with the federal government as regulations reach into local concerns; national education programs like No Child Left Behind and Common Core, for example, extensively affect local school districts.

And of course, increased capacity brings with it a higher price tag. Modernization and new technology may make it easier for governments to be more efficient, but it is pretty clear that spending has outpaced technological efficiency. Expenditures for state and local governments—our most accurate source for this data, the U.S. Census Bureau, does not separate the two—have tripled since the 1970s, placing considerable strain on local revenues, especially property taxes. And unlike the national government, local governments cannot freely borrow; they essentially need to balance their budget every year.

LOCAL GOVERNMENTS DO IMPORTANT STUFF

As I may have said a few times already, local government is all about land use. Again, *zoning* rules are a big deal and the chief way that local governments influence development within their borders. Where homes, businesses, and government offices are built can shape a community for better or for worse. Local leaders have to try and harness market forces, defend equal access to housing, promote economic development, and balance disparate interests while essentially trying to design the future of their city or county. Although doing this is not easy, it is incredibly essential to the success of a locality.

But local governments also handle a host of other issues and items in our daily lives, including:

- **Services**: one of the main things government does is provide services. Garbage pickup. Libraries and parks. Health clinics. Homeless shelters. Snow removal. Road maintenance. Animal control. Name a thing that a government might do, and local government probably does it.
- **Taxes**: all of these services, as well as the staff that provides them, are paid for through taxes. Most often, local governments rely on property taxes to fund most of their activities. (I should point out here that you do *not* have to own property to pay these taxes; they are passed on to renters, for example, through rent payments.) Along with increased capacity, though, local governments have developed a number of additional revenue streams, especially through taxes on admissions, meals, cigarettes, gas, and other forms of economic activity.
- **Public education**: as noted in the last chapter, school boards and administration are the most common single-purpose government. Most American children are educated through their local public school system, and their families are engaged with the schools for over a decade, so this remains the most common government "experience." Even if you do not have children in the public school system, a significant chunk of your tax dollars probably goes to fund it, so everyone has a stake in the success of public education.

- **Social issues**: one of the drivers of increased capacity is the expansion of political interest in social issues over the past few decades. Local governments have either decided or been forced to weigh in on controversial issues from abortion clinic regulations to anti-discrimination laws to "sanctuary city" resolutions.

If local government is so involved in so many issues, why are citizen interest and voter participation so low? Aside from the usual obstacles to engaging Americans in politics, a key problem is the lack of media coverage. Local newspapers are suffering a rapid decline, and many news sources in even the largest media markets have been subject to corporate consolidation, cuts in investigative journalism budgets, and closures. Technology like the Internet provides new opportunities for blogging, live video feeds, and online streaming from both government and private sources, but these new media do not always have the accompanying resources to gain traction among the general public. The resulting "news deserts" are a real problem for keeping people informed about what is going on in their local government.

LOCAL GOVERNMENTS ARE LOCAL

In general, if you want to have your voice heard in politics, the key things you want are **access** and **impact**. Access means you can be seen—you can get into a room with the people who actually have decision-making power. Impact means that once you get in that room, you can actually be heard—you have at least a chance of substantively affecting the outcome of laws and regulations. If you believe at all in democratic principles, then you should care about the public having opportunities for access and impact, with any government official. "Regular" citizens need to be able to participate in the decisions that affect them, at all levels of government.

But the fact is that local government is where you get the most bang for your buck. Local public officials are often part-time government actors who have "real" jobs in the community. They may even be people we know, or they at least know someone we know. You can often talk directly to local candidates running for office to find out what they think and believe, and how they are going to govern. And then when they get elected, you can often find them either in their literal offices or in their daily lives.

Here's just one example from my own life. I live in the capital city of Richmond, Virginia. In 2016, when there was a city council election, it turned out that I knew both of the main contenders in my council district. Sure, I am an active political junkie who pays attention to this stuff. But even if I hadn't been, one candidate lived down the street from me, and I had seen him around the neighborhood for years. The other candidate was our school board representative and was not only a friend of friends, but was someone I often ran into at local soccer games. This, in a city of over 200,000 people! Imagine a small town or county, where the local mayor or commissioner may be a direct acquaintance, friend, or relative.

At the local level, there are plenty of opportunities for access to decision-makers. Local council or board meetings are probably held at least every month or maybe more often; most states require these meetings to have official public comment periods, when you can speak up and be heard. But even if you cannot attend a meeting, you should not be afraid to catch the local official in public (within reason, that is, not on the way to the emergency room) or to make an appointment with them whenever they have public office hours.

You can even run for office! Sure, you probably have to collect signatures on a petition or meet up with local party officials to get on a ballot. Still, in many counties and municipalities across the country, the barrier to entry is extremely low. How low? In 2016 in Amherst, Virginia, a woman named Renell Meeks was elected to town council through a write-in campaign. She only needed 84 votes! That's hardly more than her extended family.

So far I have mentioned mostly local legislators. But even local government has an executive branch to administer and enforce the laws. For some small counties and municipalities, this could be just a tiny staff consisting of a manager and a clerk or two. A small staff can be a problem when a primitive local government hasn't caught up with the demand for services. But it also presents an opportunity in that you can get to know that clerk—again, you may know them already—to find out how things happen in your locality. Clerks are often the most "plugged in" to the local political scene as well as the most knowledgeable about how to get things done.

There may be other officials as well. In the previous chapter, I noted complaints about the "long ballot" in local government— that there may be needless elections for executive positions that should really be appointed. But if you do have those elections, you can at least take advantage of the opportunity to get to know your local tax collector or treasurer during their campaigns, or run for those positions yourself.

Just to be clear, I am not encouraging you to ply your local officials with bribes or to mercilessly stalk them! But if there is an important proposed tax cut or increase, a plan to build something, a change in school policy, or even just a need to get a permit, it helps to know the people in government and how government operates. And if you know the decision-makers, you have a chance to make your case and possibly even change the outcome. (I write more about this in the final chapter.) Thanks to the size and scope of local government, this kind of access and impact is almost easy.

So not only do the policies and choices matter in local politics, but you can actually do something about them.

SUMMARY

- The story of local governments in recent decades is one of <u>increased capacity</u>—they are doing more than ever to respond to citizen needs.
- Local government action covers <u>land use</u>, provision of <u>services</u>, <u>taxation</u>, <u>public education</u>, controversial <u>social issues</u>, and more.
- Local government does a better job than higher levels of government at providing <u>access</u> and <u>impact</u>, the ability to be seen and heard by public officials and decision-makers.

ACTION STEPS

- *Get to know your local decision-makers—legislators and administrators. (They may be people you already know.)*
- *Consider running for office—it may not take much to win!*

WANT TO KNOW MORE?

Probably every local government textbook mentions the idea of increased local government activity, but Bowman and Kearney's *State and Local Government* (again, my favorite) makes an especially big deal of the idea of "capacity." This term is borrowed from the economics and management literature, and it has been most successfully applied to government action by government economist and retired University of Cincinnati faculty member Beth Walter Honadle. If you want to dig further into capacity, she has written a lot on it; her co-edited book from 1986, *Perspectives on Management Capacity Building*, is a good place to start.

I only briefly mention policy diffusion here, but it is a common topic in studies of public policy in state and local governments; a significant part of the idea of increased capacity is the way that policies become spread among localities. You could do worse than read Charles R. Shipan and Craig Volden's oft-cited overview, "Policy Diffusion: Seven Lessons for Scholars and Practitioners."

Finally, the *Columbia Journalism Review* has been tracking news deserts on their website at https://www.cjr.org/local_news/american-news-deserts-donuts-local.php.

BIBLIOGRAPHY/FURTHER READING

Barnett, Jeffrey L., Cindy L. Sheckells, Scott Peterson, and Elizabeth M. Tydings. 2014. "2012 Census of Governments: Finance—State and Local Government Summary Report." Washington, DC: U.S. Census Bureau.

Bowman, Ann O'M., and Richard C. Kearney. 2017. *State and Local Government*. 10th ed. Boston: Cengage.

Honadle, Beth Walter. 2001. "Theoretical and Practical Issues of Local Government Capacity in an Era of Devolution." *Journal of Regional Analysis and Policy* 31 (1): 1–14.

Honadle, Beth Walter, and Arnold M. Howitt, eds. 1986. *Perspectives on Management Capacity Building*. Albany: SUNY Press.

Shipan, Charles R., and Craig Volden. 2012. "Policy Diffusion: Seven Lessons for Scholars and Practitioners." *Public Administration Review* 72 (6): 788–96.

NO TAXPAYER FUNDING FOR STADIUM/ARENA PROJECTS

Like a number of sports teams, the Washington Redskins, a professional American football team, does not actually play its games in its nominal hometown. Since 1997, home games have kicked off at a stadium in Landover, Maryland, about 10 miles east of Washington, DC. (So roughly seven hours in traffic.)

About a decade ago, the team, looking to strengthen and extend its fan base south of DC, wanted to move its summer training camp from Pennsylvania to Richmond, Virginia. In 2012, the team cut a deal with Richmond leaders to have the city build a new training facility. A year later, in 2013, the relocated training camp opened to the tremendous excitement of city leaders and fans in the area, amid loud buzz that the team's presence would draw fans—and dollars—from miles around.

And yet, just a few years later, city officials were scrambling to distance themselves from the deal. Reports of hidden costs, declining attendance, and very little income for the city were everywhere. During the 2016 citywide election, candidates for mayor were actively denouncing the deal, promising to rework or, if possible, even cancel it.

How did this happen? It turns out that projects like this—sports facilities and music venues, from a small practice field to a full-sized downtown arena or suburban stadium—almost always follow the exact same pattern. Let's run through this bite-sized example of the Richmond training camp so you can see how it works.

FANFARE

Everything usually starts with a major announcement by political officials: a sportsball team is coming to town! "Virginia considers the Redskins our team," Governor Bob McDonnell crowed in a June 2012 press release announcing the training camp location. A few months later, Richmond Mayor Dwight Jones held a press conference on the soon-to-be-developed site, complete with city officials, NFL executives, and even team cheerleaders.

Opposition to this kind of project is often disorganized or muted at the beginning, so initial media reports often credulously restate the city and team's talking points. And such points always involve *big* promises. At his 2012 presser, Mayor Jones told reporters that the training camp was "going to bring people in from all over the region to see the team play and that reverberates in economic impact for [neighborhoods], hotels, and restaurants." The city and team claimed that the camp would bring as much as $8.5 million and 100,000 fans to Richmond each year. These claims were parroted by news media, although almost always without any accompanying investigation.

URGENCY

At some point after the initial announcement, there almost always follows a suddenly urgent need to get the deal done *now*, or else it might fall apart. With the Redskins, the city administration placed tremendous pressure on Richmond City Council to make sure it approved the deal, giving council members just a few weeks for review. As the *Richmond Times Dispatch* reported in 2012, the city's chief administrator warned the council that, "It is going to take everything we can do to get this project built in seven months. . . . We are asking if at all possible to get this approved. . . . Every day is precious."

Anything could happen with a delay, boosters often claim in these cases: loan costs could increase, necessary investment partners could back out, or the sports team or league might even change its mind. (What these boosters typically do not mention is their worst-case scenario: the public might start examining the deal in more detail and start to realize it's a sucker bet. But we will get to that.)

The Richmond City Council, worried about blocking a deal that would bring money and jobs to the city, approved the Redskins training camp in a unanimous vote. But it happened so quickly that there was very little public input; in fact, the council barely understood what they were voting for, as city residents quickly learned.

RAPID DECLINE

The camp opened in 2013, and everything was great—for a year or two. The opening day attendance numbers set a Redskins training camp record, and the first two years were record-setting as well. However, even these numbers were collected and reported solely by the team, which has a history of possible exaggeration. (A 2018 report, published on the *Deadspin* sports website, alleged that the Redskins had lied for years about a supposedly immense waiting list for season-ticket holders, apparently just making up numbers as they went along.) In fact, most media reports at the time either ignored or glossed over the fact that the team counted fans who attended morning and afternoon practice sessions *twice*, so that the attendance numbers had possibly been overestimated by as much as 100 percent. But even with these goosed numbers, attendance soon declined precipitously. By the fourth year of the training camp, the team stopped even releasing their attendance figures. It turns out that not as many people as promised wanted to come and watch large men in plastic hit each other for a few weeks in summer.

UGLY DETAILS

It was not just attendance numbers that became a problem. For example, the training camp was originally hyped as a boon to local restaurants, as visitors would surely flock to the city's growing food scene. Instead, football fans mostly purchased food from vendors inside the camp, with money going directly to Redskins ownership. Mindful of the growing bad press, the team worked with the city to set up a food court near the camp, staffed by local food trucks, but the area failed to generate much in the way of customer traffic or business, especially as overall attendance dropped.

But wait, there's more: the Redskins reduced the number of days the camp was open. When another team, the New England Patriots, came to town for joint practices, they stayed at a suburban hotel, providing tax revenue to nearby Henrico County instead of the City of Richmond. Police officers were required to provide additional staff time for camp security at an estimated annual cost of $40,000, all on the city's dime.

And that is before we even get to the role of the named sponsor in the deal, Bon Secours Health Services. This Maryland-based healthcare system operates a number of hospitals and clinics in the Richmond area; they ponied up money for naming rights to the football camp and committed to expanding healthcare services for low-income residents in the East End of Richmond. To Bon

Secours's credit, it followed through on the latter by opening a "healthy living center" on the city's Nine Mile Road in 2017. Named for Sarah Garland Jones, Virginia's first African American and female doctor, the center offers group therapy, nutrition counseling, and wellness therapies to the East End's mostly black population.

But Bon Secours also committed to renovating two beloved historic school buildings in the city's West End to be used by the hospital system to train nurses. When these renovations turned out to be too expensive, the system planned to instead raze both buildings, using a mixed-use development plan to fund new construction. After a loud public outcry (Virginians know a thing or two about history), the city council managed to negotiate a plan with the hospital system to preserve at least the older of the two buildings. But because of the delays caused by these planning hiccups and resulting negotiations, construction on the site began only in 2019—*six years* after originally projected.

TAXPAYERS MAKE UP THE DIFFERENCE

Issues with the hospital facility's construction were more than just a problem for historical preservationists. Property tax revenue from the project was supposed to fund the city's payments to the team. Yes, you read that right: not only did the city agree to develop and renovate the training camp facility, but the deal also required a subsidy to the team just for the right to host the camp! City administrators eventually reported that this subsidy, plus debt payments on the loan necessary to fund the new training facility, amounted to well over $1 million each year.

In 2018, the city council was forced to refinance this loan as the property tax revenue from the Bon Secours hospital facilities fell far short of projections. How much the training camp cost the city depends on how you count, but the amount is clearly over hundreds of thousands of dollars per year. A January 2019 report from the

Center for Urban and Regional Analysis at Virginia Commonwealth University suggested that the city *might* break even in 2023, with an eventual net positive for the deal over its long, long life. But that report admittedly relies on assumptions that the hospital system will keep its construction commitments and renew its naming rights agreements, not to mention some possibly problematic assumptions about economic impact (which we'll get to below).

The current deal runs through 2020. But even if the city just drops out of it—and it may—debt payments on the loan will continue through 2033. So the city has some incentive to try to stay in business with the team that fleeced it, just to recoup its initial costs.

So, just to recap what happened here: public officials told citizens that it was a good idea to build a sports facility, promising millions of dollars of "impact" and tons of jobs. They rushed the deal through before any organized opposition could form or the public could scrutinize the deal in any substantive way. Then, almost immediately, the ugly details started revealing themselves: hidden costs, fewer benefits than officials foretold, and broken promises. Taxpayers ended up on the hook for years.

This is a training facility of one of the most powerful sports leagues in the country, but you do not need a greedy NFL owner or sports team involved to have the same exact story play out in your city or county. Of course, the stakes, and the numbers, are raised when it comes to a sports stadium or multi-purpose arena. Hundreds of millions of dollars are spent, followed by the same delusions, lies, and eventual regret. This tale of woe is repeated over and over again in cities and counties across the country. Here's hoping it doesn't happen to *you*.

WHY DOES THIS HAPPEN?

Why do we see this happen over and over, even though people should really know by now that it is a bad deal?

It is not hard to figure out the perspective of the developers and owners and why they may try to get the best deal possible for themselves. Facilities make a lot of money for sports team owners and other owner-operators, particularly if these facilities are configured with "luxury suites" and all the amenities high-income fans expect from a sports or concert experience. But the pressure on developers to get a good deal from localities has increased especially as the at-home experience has grown better and better. High-definition televisions mean that sports like hockey are no longer difficult to follow on a screen. Sports like football may be even better: you can have a great fan experience at home or at the bar instead of paying $100 for parking, freezing at the game, and taking hours to drive home in traffic. Similarly, concert films, streaming and YouTube, and the wide availability of all kinds of music may make catching a live show of a touring band less alluring. Now more than ever, owners and developers are feeling the need to squeeze every dollar they can out of their properties.

On the other hand, sports fans can find it difficult to take a hard line on a team's stadium demands. Team owners often come from successful business backgrounds, and they seem to almost intuitively recognize the importance of *leverage*. The ability of a local sports team to pull up stakes and find a willing suitor in another locality or even another state gives owners tons of this leverage. They know that local public officials do *not* want to be blamed for "forcing" the local baseball or hockey team to move to Alaska. If the owner can get a new stadium or arena to play in without having to pay for it, then why not play hardball with the local mayor or board of supervisors? (This is one more example of the insidious pressure a fleeing business can put on local governments, as we'll see in the later chapter on regional cooperation.)

Sports fandom is a weird thing, for sure, but anyone who has been to a Cleveland Browns game knows how persistent it can be in the face of all rational thought. (Sorry, Browns fans.)

Psychologically, fandom can lead citizens to weigh the cost of stadium and arena deals much differently from other taxpayers. And even if a resident is not a sports fan, they may buy into some idea of civic identity or "civic pride." Having a sizeable downtown arena where national music acts come to play, or having a team from one of the major professional sports leagues, can in some ineffable way define your locality as a "real" place. It can be a giant blow to the collective ego of a city if it loses a team—just ask Seattle about the Sonics or Hartford, Connecticut, about whether they miss the Mighty Whale.

Public officials are working under other incentives as well. For example, a number of political scientists have studied political coalition-building in urban areas. Although they differ on what exactly is the best way to explain how it works, most agree that (again) land development dominates local politics. This is true in part because private interests that own real estate have an especially powerful economic incentive to work with city leaders to spur economic development: growth of the city ensures growth in the worth of their property investments. And local government gains much from working with landowners to promote this development as well. Sociologist Harvey Molotch even quoted the term "growth machine" to describe this mode of local politics that is focused on economic growth through the development of buildings and land.

The power of local landowners has only been enhanced as businesses have become more mobile in a truly global economy. A corporation can get a sweet development deal from the city by threatening to move its offices or factory to another city or state. But an equally powerful company in a city or county, such as the local developer that owns the industrial park or shopping mall in town, may be the one that stays. These developers, as well as utility companies, hospital corporations, and other "fixed-place" business interests, may have a real estate portfolio and a network of local contacts, vendors and suppliers, and political connections that make moving costly to impossible. But those networks and portfolios make them powerful actors in local politics in the long term. Some scholars, led by urban theorist Clarence Stone, even suggest that these local business leaders join with political elites to form a ruling "regime" that lasts over multiple elections, officials, and administrations.

And so a sports team or development group that wants to transform a "blighted" or underused area of town into a new arena can often find it relatively easy to get public officials dreaming big. Based on the "growth machine" idea, city leaders are primed to listen; based on the "regime" idea, these powerful landowners may already be a part of the influential elites who set the political agenda in a city or county.

We should never forget, also, that city leaders are actual human beings, with psychological needs of their own. You do not have to be a Freudian analyst to recognize that everyone wants to make their mark on the world, and politicians may be more driven by the idea of legacy than anyone. Seeing their name on a plaque in a building lobby or on a sign outside a new park—or, yes, on the walls of an arena or stadium—helps a mayor or county supervisor know that no matter their faults or failures, they have accomplished *something* in this world. And then, of course, there are political benefits as well. As journalist Mike Royko once wrote about how Chicago Mayor Richard J. Daley worked, "The fastest way to show people that something is happening is to build things." A construction project is a tangible example of political power and accomplishment, even if the community may suffer from it in the long term.

One final contributor to the prevalence of bad deals is the time frame involved. With the Redskins training camp example above, the city's mayor and administrative staff, who negotiated the deal, plus many of the council members who approved it, were no longer in office by the time the full details were revealed. A central principle of democracy is the ability to hold leaders accountable for their actions. But for development deals like a new arena or stadium, those leaders are often long gone by the time the bill comes due.

HOW BAD A DEAL IS IT?

One way to see if a policy or plan is a good idea is to conduct a **cost–benefit analysis**. If the benefits are greater than the costs, then you can go ahead with a clear conscience. Unfortunately, for most publicly financed stadium and arena projects, this kind of analysis almost always produces the same results. Early estimates *understate* the actual costs, as the players involved have significant incentives to minimize expenses to ensure the deal is signed. The benefits are then almost always *overestimated*, but it may take years or even decades for citizens to finally figure out that the promised results are never going to materialize. Let's look at each of these—costs and benefits—in turn.

Underestimated Costs

If you are wondering how often and by how much stadium and arena projects typically underestimate costs, here are just a few examples:

- A 2017 audit of the construction of a minor league baseball stadium in Nashville, Tennessee, revealed that a project originally estimated to cost $65 million had ballooned to over $90 million. Why? According to the audit, early estimates "were based on a two-year-old feasibility study and did not factor in a compressed design and construction schedule to complete the project for the Spring 2015 season opening game." Even better: the original proposals forgot to mention that the surrounding area would need $20 million in required infrastructure improvements. (Oops.)

- In March of 2018, the *Washington City Paper* reported that a 4,200-seat basketball arena and practice facility built in the DC area for the NBA's Wizards, WNBA's Mystics, and minor league Capital City Go-Go would need significantly more money than anticipated solely due to increased basic construction costs, like supplies and labor. In fact, the budget rose 25 percent from originally approved estimates, from $55 million to almost $70 million. Taxpayers were going to have to foot the bill: thanks to the deal negotiated by city leaders, any cost overruns had to be covered by city restaurant and hotel taxes.

- In August 2002, the Houston Texans triumphantly debuted Reliant Stadium, the first NFL facility with a retractable roof; two years later, they hosted the city's first Super Bowl in three decades. Unfortunately, by the end of the decade, the sports authority (a single-purpose government) that financed the stadium was being bailed out by local governments for millions of dollars, a year after the national economic crisis forced it to restructure its debt. By 2018, the still-significant bond debt was being audited by the IRS for possibly violating tax laws, while the tax revenues that were supposed to pay off the bonds had not hit their projected totals for years. Oh, and after hosting a second Super Bowl in 2017, local boosters were already talking about the need for costly upgrades.

- In case you thought these were recent problems, *The New York Times* reported in November of 1979 that the Meadowlands Arena construction project, which would eventually host both the basketball Nets and hockey Devils, was already over budget by $20 million thanks to "an overly ambitious construction-cost estimate" from the developers.

- Of course, it could be worse: you could end up hosting the Olympic games, which, according to Clay Dillow of the analytics website *FiveThirtyEight*, may be the worst stadium bet going. According to Dillow's analysis, the *average* cost overrun for Olympic facilities is *90 percent*!

Here's the thing: we should *expect* ballooning budgets. According to engineers, cost overruns have become almost a natural part of *all* major construction projects. But often with stadium and arena proposals, particularly those involving sports teams, everyone—local officials, the media, and citizens—just accepts developers' initial estimates without question. Instead, negotiations for construction need to assume a reasonable amount of overage, then determine who is going to pay for it ahead of time.

Overestimated Benefits

While costs often rise, we have the opposite problem on the benefits side: the rosy scenarios projected by developers and boosters rarely come true.

To make the case for building a stadium or arena, teams and city boosters often turn to **economic impact assessments**. This kind of study bolsters the idea that a new facility will spur economic activity in the locality that hosts it. People from all over will come to town for the game or concert and also spend money on hotels, restaurants, and goods in the area. This increased commercial activity supports local businesses, creates jobs to handle the additional business, and contributes to the local government's tax revenues. However, there are many, many reasons to be skeptical of these kinds of claims.

First, boosters often point to a one-time "direct" economic impact from construction. For big-time stadium projects, this can reach a billion dollars or more, which sounds like a huge number—and it is! But we need to remember that this includes the *spending* on the project. You can count any investment from a team or private developers as "impactful" spending, sure. But impact estimates also include the millions in public funds that are often needed to finance infrastructure improvements or that sometimes even go to a team in the form of tax incentives. By sliding initial spending on construction, infrastructure, and incentives onto the benefits side, this economic model essentially translates costs into benefits. Literally *everything* becomes an economic "impact."

For example, an "impact summary" prepared by the Southern Nevada Tourism Infrastructure Committee on a proposed pro football stadium in Las Vegas touted the project's $1.7 billion in "One-Time Impacts during Construction." This report, prepared during the 2016–18 stadium frenzy, when Vegas successfully lured the Raiders from California, neglected to mention that much of these construction costs would be financed by taxpayers. In the end, Las Vegas officials arranged for over $700 million in public funds to help pay for the Raiders to begin playing in Las Vegas. Should these taxpayer funds—which now cannot go to pay for schools, roads, or anything else—really count as a benefit or a cost?

And that's not all: impact assessments often do a bad job with the space–time continuum, condensing years or even decades of construction into a much shorter period, even (if only by implication) a single year. For example, a study could calculate the economic impact of construction, add in the effects of the resulting facilities/ventures, then consolidate all of this into a bottom-line "Total Economic Impact," as if everything magically appeared at once. But as we have already seen, construction estimates are already optimistic in terms of costs, often wildly so; they also tend to underestimate project timelines. Even if everything goes as planned, full-scale construction often takes years to reach completion. The "$1 billion in impact!" as claimed by analysts, or more often, the officials and boosters who want to build, should more accurately be spread over years, if not decades.

And few, if any, of these impact analyses mention any separate costs associated with the project that offset the benefits. Whereas it is true that a developed property will likely bring in more economic activity and tax revenue than an empty lot, it may also require more public spending for infrastructure and services. Maybe you need a new traffic light, increased police and fire protection, or more teachers and classroom space as families move in. One 2011 study of a sports project (albeit involving an international sporting event, not a stadium), which was sold to taxpayers for its economic impact, argued that an actual cost–benefit analysis showed a net loss for the local economy and suggested that many other projects would show the same loss if we paid more attention to costs.

Similarly, for all the supposed economic impacts from facility construction and use, there often is no accounting for existing revenues from the area, otherwise known as the "do-nothing option." How much, if any, of the supposedly new economic activity—and resulting tax revenue—would happen without the development? Stadium and arena developers often propose to build in "empty" or "blighted" areas, but sometimes they redevelop existing neighborhoods or hop on board an already fast-moving train in a "hot" section of town. Similarly, impact studies rarely take into account "opportunity costs," an economic term that refers to the lost opportunities from spending money on one thing instead of another. Every dollar spent on an arena is one fewer dollar used for government services, staff, and programs. It can be even more difficult than usual for a city or county to find money for a new soccer field or basketball court, a new health clinic to combat drug addiction, or even raises for police officers, if all their money is tied up in stadium construction. And yet all of these other government functions also have impacts, economic or otherwise.

Overall, economists are generally skeptical of the effects of arenas and stadiums on local economies. One well-cited evaluation of sports facilities was offered in a 1997 Brookings study and subsequent book by economists Roger G. Noll and Andrew Zimbalist. Their primary conclusion about economic impact: sports stadiums do *not* bring in new money from outside a locality but mostly displace spending from other local entertainment sources. (Economists sometimes call this the "substitution effect.") Many other economists agree: sports facilities do not generate much in economic development or tax revenue—certainly not enough to cover their costs in any reasonable way.

Local governments could limit their risk by not handing out huge tax incentives or making extensive commitments to spending their own dollars on infrastructure improvements. Of course, it makes some general sense for localities to entice developers to build a project by offering moderate tax breaks or other incentives. But Timothy J. Bartik, an economist at Michigan think tank Upjohn Institute, argues that most local government incentives, even for smaller projects, are actually wasted. According to Bartik's 2018 white paper, incentives only "tip" development projects over the edge into materialization 20 percent of the time; the rest of the time, whether development will happen or not depends on other factors completely independent of the incentives offered. And yet, local governments seem desperate to hand out public dollars to the latest shiny project, especially if a sportsball is involved.

WHAT SHOULD WE DO ABOUT IT?

The first thing localities should do to avoid these problems may be obvious: resist. Do not answer the siren call of developers and sports owners who have a "great deal" for the city or county, whether they are outsiders coming from elsewhere or folks who already make their home there. If an area does have a team or arena knocking on its door, local officials should at least negotiate a better deal than others have in the past.

This is actually possible. When the Rams football team moved from St. Louis to Los Angeles in 2016, team owner Stan Kroenke paid most of the bill for a new, multi-billion-dollar stadium. Los Angeles ended up giving at least $150 million in dedicated sales tax contributions, but that's much less than the $450-million package that St. Louis offered for the Rams to stay home. (Poor St. Louis is still forking over millions per year just to pay off its old stadium, even with the Rams now living it up on the West Coast.) Two decades earlier, when Seattle gave the baseball Mariners millions to help build a new ballpark, it made sure to include in the deal that the team would cover any construction cost overruns. Even so, the city still essentially had to sue the team to make sure it paid the $100-million tab; it helped that the Mariners' owners angered star player Ken Griffey Jr. by insinuating that the construction bill would prevent them from being able to afford to pay him. Still, it was a victory for Seattle taxpayers when the team eventually had to pay up.

Seattle is actually an excellent example of how a city can not only negotiate better deals, but completely refuse a bad one. In 2006, a citizen advocacy group with the terrific name of Citizens for More Important Things got voters to approve an initiative that prevents Seattle government from signing development deals unless the developers can prove that there will be a better return on investment than U.S. Treasury bonds. Not every city or county has the same robust initiative process that the state of Washington does, but voters elsewhere can at least start by getting local officials to demand similar accounting proof.

Even folks in the city of Richmond, Virginia, with whom we started off this chapter, may have learned something from their NFL training camp debacle. Even as the Redskins camp was opening, Mayor Dwight Jones also proposed building a minor league baseball stadium downtown to replace the aging Diamond ballpark in another part of the city. Residents quickly rallied against the $80-million proposal, and eventually the mayor with-drew the plan before the Richmond City Council could vote it down. Yet another proposal by the next mayor for a downtown arena development was also voted down by the council in early 2020 after strong public opposition. Cities like Richmond are learning to say "no."

It is true that once in a while a locality can get lucky with a stadium deal. Take Durham, North Carolina, which spent almost $20 million on the Durham Bulls Athletic Park in 1995 and contributed millions more to renovations for the ballpark in 2014. The "D-Bap," as locals call it, is widely considered to have kicked off a renaissance in the downtown American Tobacco Historic District, with restaurants and bars, a performing arts center, and hundreds of new apartments rising up in the years since. The city is still paying for the stadium, but most officials and citizens are totally comfortable with that bill. Still, even in Durham, it can be hard to say how much credit the baseball stadium should get for the downtown revitalization. The arts center required another $30 million in public funds, plus the area received significant additional investments from the baseball team's parent company, which bought and renovated an aging tobacco factory, as well as from nearby Duke University. Without these supporting contri-butions, it is quite possible that the stadium would never have produced such prominent effects.

Still, even if you want to give the baseball team all of the credit in the world, Durham is the exception that proves the rule. In most cases, localities that devote millions to building a sports facility or arena of any kind end up regretting it much more than Durham residents do. Public officials who control purse strings should be extra careful about how much they give away to developers and owners. Media organizations and citizens need to treat any claims about "economic impact" with extreme skepticism. Big, shiny projects like sports arenas are exciting and fun, and may even be profitable—at least for their owners. But if the private sector does not seem to think it is worth the cost to build these projects unless they receive huge public subsidies, then it is probably not worth it for taxpayers either.

SUMMARY

- Stadium and arena projects almost always follow the same pattern: <u>fanfare</u>, <u>rushed deals</u>, and then <u>ugly details and regrets</u>.
- City leaders sign on to bad stadium deals thanks to sports teams' <u>leverage</u> and promises of <u>economic impact</u> on businesses and tax revenue.
- Most economic impact studies <u>underestimate costs</u> and <u>overestimate benefits</u>.
- Localities can <u>negotiate better deals</u> and even <u>say "no."</u>

ACTION STEPS

- *Be skeptical of claims about economic impact.*
- *Reject public financing for stadium and arena projects.*

WANT TO KNOW MORE?

As I suggested at the end of this book's first chapter, the story of stadium financing begins and ends with journalist Neil deMause. His *Field of Schemes* website remains absolutely essential, and many of his arguments were summed up in a 1999 book of the same name (updated in 2015).

You can also find tons of academic research on stadium studies if you are so inclined. One good economic study is the aforementioned *Sports, Jobs and Taxes* from Brookings economists Noll and Zimbalist. The 2003 book *Public Dollars, Private Stadiums* is a solid introduction to the problem from a sociological perspective. For more general studies on how local politics bends toward land use and development, you could start with *Urban Fortunes* by John

Logan and Harvey Molotch, based on Molotch's classic 1976 article on "growth machines." (I recommend the book's 20th anniversary edition published in 2007.) I also mentioned above Clarence Stone's "regime analysis" theory, most famously articulated in his 1989 book *Regime Politics*.

Conservatives have criticized public subsidies from a libertarian perspective for decades. A classic statement on the issue is the Cato Institute's 1999 report *Sports Pork: The Costly Relationship between Major League Sports and Government*. More recently, the conservative think tank Heartland Institute has taken up the cause, with policy analyst Matthew Glans offering a nice round-up of research in a 2018 commentary.

If you really want to get technical, you can find more specialized information on general cost overruns for construction projects in Israeli engineering professor Yehiel Rosenfeld's academic article "Root-Cause Analysis of Construction-Cost Overruns" in the *Journal of Construction Engineering and Management*.

Whereas arenas are not always about sports, fandom plays a significant role in public support for bad stadium deals. Eric Simons's 2013 book *The Secret Lives of Sports Fans* is an entertaining journalistic account that combines science with fan experience. For the drier, more academic stuff, try 2019's *Sport Fans: The Psychology and Social Impact of Fandom*, edited by two psychologists.

Finally, since I started this chapter with a story about the Washington professional football team, I cannot finish it without noting that the team's name is a racial slur. Many fans do not seem to care much, and the owner has dug in, defending the name. But you can find many, many resources from academics and advocates to explain why the name should be changed: you could start with the website of the National Congress of American Indians (www.ncai.org), especially with its page on "Anti-Defamation & Mascots."

BIBLIOGRAPHY/FURTHER READING

Bartik, Timothy. 2018. "'But For' Percentages for Economic Development Incentives: What Percentage Estimates Are Plausible Based on the Research Literature?" Upjohn Institute Working Papers, January. https://doi.org/10.17848/wp18-289.

Center for Urban and Regional Analysis. 2019. "Bon Secours Redskins: Economic and Fiscal Impact of Training Camp and Associated Development." Richmond, VA: VCU Center for Urban and Regional Analysis.

Delaney, Kevin J., and Rick Eckstein. 2003. *Public Dollars, Private Stadiums: The Battle Over Building Sports Stadiums*. New Brunswick, NJ: Rutgers University Press.

deMause, Neil, and Joanna Cagan. 2015. *Field of Schemes: How the Great Stadium Swindle Turns Public Money into Private Profit*, Revised and Expanded Edition. Lincoln: University of Nebraska Press.

DeVane, Steve. 2017. "How Durham's Ballpark Triggered a Downtown Renaissance." *The Fayetteville Observer*. August 19. https://www.fayobserver.com/news/20170819/how-durhams-ballpark-triggered-downtown-renaissance.

Dillow, Clay. 2016. "Hosting the Olympics Is a Terrible Investment." *FiveThirtyEight*. August 15. https://fivethirtyeight.com/features/hosting-the-olympics-is-a-terrible-investment/.

Edwards, Suzanne. 2015. "What Those Stadiums Cost You: Sports Authority Refinances Debt." *Houston Business Journal*. January 7. https://www.bizjournals.com/houston/morning_call/2015/01/what-those-stadiums-cost-you-sports-authority.html.

Giambrone, Andrew. 2018. "Price Tag of Taxpayer-Funded Wizards Arena Grows to $69 Million." *Washington City Paper*. March 1. https://www.washingtoncitypaper.com/news/loose-lips/blog/20994367/price-tag-of-taxpayerfunded-wizards-arena-grows-to-69-million.

Glans, Matthew. 2018. "Bad Stadium Deals Hurt Cities Large and Small." *Heartland Institute*. September 25. https://www.heartland.org/publications-resources/publications/research--commentary-bad-stadium-deals-hurt-cities-large-and-small.

Hanley, Robert. 1979. "$27.4 Million in Overruns for Meadowlands Arena." *The New York Times*, November 21. https://www.nytimes.

com/1979/11/21/archives/274-million-in-overruns-for-meadowlands-arena-342-million-for.html.

Keating, Raymond J. 1999. "Sports Pork: The Costly Relationship between Major League Sports and Government." *Cato Institute*. April 5. https://www.cato.org/publications/policy-analysis/sports-pork-costly-relationship-between-major-league-sports-government.

Logan, John R., and Harvey Luskin Molotch. 2007. *Urban Fortunes: The Political Economy of Place*. Berkeley: University of California Press.

Metropolitan Nashville Office of Internal Audit. 2017. "Audit of the First Tennessee Ballpark Construction Project." Revised Edition. Nashville, TN: Metropolitan Nashville Office of Internal Audit.

Molotch, Harvey. 1976. "The City as a Growth Machine: Toward a Political Economy of Place." *American Journal of Sociology* 82 (2): 309–32.

Noll, Roger G., and Andrew Zimbalist, eds. 1997. *Sports, Jobs, and Taxes: The Economic Impact of Sports Teams and Stadiums*. Washington, DC: Brookings Institution Press.

Rosenfeld, Yehiel. 2014. "Root-Cause Analysis of Construction-Cost Overruns." *Journal of Construction Engineering and Management* 140 (1): 04013039. https://doi.org/10.1061/(ASCE)CO.1943-7862.0000789.

Royko, Mike. 1988. *Boss: Richard J. Daley of Chicago*. New York: Plume.

Simons, Eric. 2013. *The Secret Lives of Sports Fans*. New York: Harry N. Abrams.

Smith, Brian T. 2017. "Facing the Reality of NRG Stadium Upgrades." *Houston Chronicle*. February 12. https://www.houstonchronicle.com/sports/columnists/smith/article/Facing-the-reality-of-NRG-Stadium-upgrades-10926138.php.

Southern Nevada Tourism Infrastructure Committee. 2017. "Impact Summary: Las Vegas Stadium." Las Vegas, NV: Southern Nevada Tourism Infrastructure Committee.

Stone, Clarence Nathan. 1989. *Regime Politics: Governing Atlanta, 1946–1988*. Lawrence: University Press of Kansas.

Taks, Marijke, Stefan Kesenne, Laurence Chalip, Christine Green, and Scott Martyn. 2011. "Economic Impact Analysis versus Cost Benefit Analysis: The Case of a Medium-Sized Sport Event." *International Journal of Sport Finance* 6 (3): 187–203.

Moomaw, Graham. 2014. "Mayor Withdraws Shockoe Ballpark Proposal." *Richmond Times-Dispatch*. May 27. https://www.richmond.com/news/local/city-of-richmond/mayor-withdraws-shockoe-ballpark-proposal/article_3e1faf7a-e5e9-11e3-87a1-0017a43b2370.html.

Wann, Daniel L., and Jeffrey D. James. 2019. *Sport Fans: The Psychology and Social Impact of Fandom*. New York: Routledge.

Zimbalist, Andrew, and Roger G. Noll. 1997. "Sports, Jobs, & Taxes: Are New Stadiums Worth the Cost?" *Brookings*. June 1. https://www.brookings.edu/articles/sports-jobs-taxes-are-new-stadiums-worth-the-cost/.

KEEP HOUSING AFFORDABLE

This may not exactly be insightful, but it's true: having a home is really, really important.

A home is valuable for all sorts of reasons, not all of which are obvious until your access to housing is threatened. We in America often play up the idea of *ownership* of a home with a car in the garage and the picket fence out front, and the whole 1950s-era suburban lifestyle is still burned into our collective imagination. Housing is actually much more diverse than that, ranging from condos to duplexes to mansions. But although around two-thirds of Americans are homeowners of some kind or another, with all the attendant benefits, housing is more than just ownership; not everyone chooses to own a home or can afford to do so.

Rather than ownership, housing is more about having a stable, clean, and secure environment, so that we can be active and productive members of society. We cannot be fully engaged citizens if we are worried about safety or about where we will end up that year, month, or evening. In fact, being "housed" provides benefits that go well beyond just having a place to put your stuff. People with stable homes are less likely to commit or fall victim to crimes, need public assistance, or lose their jobs. Lack of a stable home can dramatically affect mental health. And owning a home is one of the best ways for lower-income and middle-class Americans to build wealth.

Some human rights advocates even argue that housing is a fundamental right. The United Nations' Universal Declaration of Human Rights includes housing among the things a person needs for "health and well-being," and it is included among other rights in a bunch of international documents that provide the basis for human rights law. Guess what? If the U.N. needs to mention something as a right that needs protection, it is a safe bet that this thing is threatened or inaccessible for many. And that is definitely the case with housing.

In fact, because its effects are so wide-ranging and significant, the lack of stable housing for all is one of our most fundamental concerns as a society. It is a challenge that belongs to everyone and every level of government. But it is often local communities and governments that have the most impact on housing affordability and availability; they also shoulder the greatest burden. Housing is impacted directly by land use, and—as you should probably know by now—land use is what local government is all about. And so a key challenge for cities and counties is making housing affordable for *all* of their citizens.

THE PROBLEM OF HOUSING

Traditionally, housing is seen as a binary problem: you either have it or you don't. And so the chief problem in this area is often seen as **homelessness**, or lack of housing, often caused by a sudden personal economic crisis or a more persistent problem like drug addiction or mental illness.

But the issue of housing is much broader than homelessness. Many people technically have homes that they can go to, but that are neither stable nor affordable. Housing advocates have more recently pushed for the idea of **housing insecurity** to widen the scope of concern. They want us to recognize that many of our most vulnerable citizens may not technically be homeless but still do not have a clean, safe home they can count on in the long term. And building enough **affordable housing** (the term most often used to talk about the problem of housing) ensures that everyone, no matter their income level, has a good place to live.

Combatting housing insecurity is one of the key solutions to poverty. Having a stable home makes employment easier: it is harder to hold down a job if you are not sure where you are going to find a bed at night, and most employers require their employees to have a fixed address. Stable and safe housing also reduces crime, in the sense that you are less likely to both be a victim and be incentivized to commit criminal acts. And there is plenty of evidence that a lack of stable housing contributes to negative health outcomes, maybe for obvious reasons. It is not just the lack of access to or affordability of healthcare that probably accompanies housing insecurity, but just the mental stress of lacking an affordable home is damaging to your health.

Even if there were not such obvious costs and benefits for individuals, there is a broad economic argument for making housing affordable. If you want to build a thriving local economy, you of course want to have plenty of high-wage jobs for "high-skilled" employees who can contribute to your tax rolls. But you also want a steady supply of workers of *all* skill and wage levels. A functioning economy needs tradespeople as well as tech workers, and service employees as well as professionals. If you want all of these workers to be productive and happy, you want them to be able to live in accessible, stable homes.

There are corresponding political and moral cases for affordable housing as well. Diverse neighborhoods are less stratified and segregated—by class, sure, but also by all the other demographic divisions that go along with class, especially race. One way to overcome the divides between ourselves and others who are different is to be literal neighbors. And then, of course, making sure everyone in your locality has a safe place to live is just the right thing to do; if we care at all about equity and inclusion, affordable housing has to be an important goal.

So with all of these arguments for and benefits of affordable housing, it is probably not good that the word that is used most often when describing how we are doing on this problem is "crisis." Cities like New York and San Francisco have exploding rents and face massive housing shortages, even for their middle-class residents. But it is not just major cities that are confronted by this crisis—small towns and rural areas are facing some of the same issues. And the problem is accelerating: the nonprofit Urban Institute argued in a 2017 report that the housing crunch had only gotten worse since 2000, especially for the poorest renters and especially in urban centers. Some economists see the data as more mixed, but even these more optimistic folks agree that the country's neediest residents, almost all of whom are renters, are getting squeezed.

A few different factors are driving the housing crisis, including the following:

- **General economic trends** have put pressure on the entire housing ecosystem. For example, wages have remained low for decades, leading to less home-buying power for consumers. More renters mean higher rents, which put homes even further out of reach in an accelerating cycle. Seemingly unrelated costs can contribute to the problem too: rising medical expenses, for instance, are a leading driver of homelessness and housing insecurity. The decline of federal subsidies for housing in recent decades does not help either.

- **Local zoning and development laws** in many areas of the country do not incentivize housing density and diversity, instead favoring the development of single-family homes with large footprints. Why? Aside from the 1950s cultural model being dominant as noted above, these single-family homes bring more profit to developers and are viewed by local officials as providing stronger and safer contributions to tax bases. Local governments are more focused on short-term gains (more taxes, good political relations with powerful developers) than long-term costs (lack of affordable housing in general).

- **Gentrification** is an especially thorny problem for local communities. This term refers to the revitalization of a "blighted" neighborhood as more affluent people move into it, bringing about renovated homes and new economic activity. This kind of neighborhood development can be a signal of a recovering local economy, but it almost always pushes out long-term, low-income residents who can no longer afford the neighborhood in which they were raised. Localities understandably welcome new economic activity and an increased tax base, but often do not do enough to help the displaced.

- **Cultural changes** have moved people away from home ownership and toward renting—especially millennials and Generation Zers, who like the amenities and flexibility. Thanks to the wage problem, though, they also probably cannot afford a sizeable down payment for home ownership. Still, there is nothing wrong with this preference except that the influx of renters again puts pressure on the entire system, especially since there is a mismatch in available housing stock.

The result of all of these overlapping pressures is an increasing number of localities where people have to move far outside of economic centers to find a place they can afford to live. Middle- and lower-income residents alike are forced to choose between the jobs they want and having a tolerable commute. Worse, many struggling families on the lower end of the income spectrum end up in subpar housing or have to constantly move from poorly maintained rentals to motels. These kinds of emergency "shelters" end up being costly for them in the long run, preventing them from building up their savings and credit history for longer-term housing and economic stability.

Underlying all of these factors is fear—namely, wealthy residents' fear that opening up their neighborhoods to affordable housing will bring lower property values, increased crime, and even higher taxes to pay for more services, like schools and welfare. In 2001, economist William Fischel coined the term **homevoter** to describe how homeowners influence municipal zoning laws and other local regulations through this economic lens. Fischel saw the preeminence of homevoters as good for political engagement and economic efficiency, but his model suggests that a sizeable minority of renters might find their own interests overwhelmed by their more powerful home-owning neighbors.

Some studies show that even the term "housing" generates negative associations for many Americans because of the long, complicated and—as always in America—racialized history of public housing. Despite the fact that data shows that truly mixed and diverse housing rarely, if ever, suffers from any of the problems that drive homevoters' fears about crime and damaged property values, the myths persist. The result is concentrated poverty in remote urban areas, away from economic development, and jobs in suburbs that are far from the people who need and want them.

WHAT'S "AFFORDABLE"?

Before we can approach any solutions, it may help to know what "affordable" even means. "Affordable" is, to use a technical term, a squishy concept; in general, different people can have very different ideas about household budgets and the appropriate amount to spend on anything.

For years, however, housing discussions have been based on a widely accepted rule of thumb: an affordable home is one that requires no more than 30 percent of a family's income. This 30 percent rule goes back to the 1968 Fair Housing Act, which was passed by Congress to limit racial discrimination in home rental and ownership. A 1969 amendment to this act first capped public housing costs at 25 percent of income, the idea being that anything over that amount would be too much of a burden for the poor. The cap was raised to 30 percent in 1981, presumably to control costs. Economists debate whether this 30 percent threshold really makes any sense, but the rule of thumb has stuck.

And by "stuck," I mean the 30 percent rule is enshrined in federal law. The Department of Housing and Urban Development (HUD) uses statistical analysis to determine what it calls the Affordable Median Income, or AMI, of an area (typically a county or city). The idea is that one half of the families in the area earn more than—and the other half less than—this number. HUD then uses the AMI to determine three groups of need, with "extremely low income" set at 30 percent AMI and below, with adjustments for family size. So, local governments eventually can get a table that looks like this:

Hypothetical Affordable Housing Table
(Adopted from MN Metro Council's 2018 Local Planning Handbook)

Household Size	Extremely Low Income (30% AMI)	Very Low Income (50% AMI)	Low Income (80% AMI)
1	$19,000	$31,650	$47,600
2	$21,700	$36,200	$54,400
3	$24,400	$40,700	$61,200
4	$27,100	$45,200	$68,000
5	$29,300	$48,850	$73,450
6	$32,960	$52,450	$78,900

Table 1

So, for this example, affordable housing rates would amount to 30 percent of the income levels in the table. This seems complicated, but you just need a little math. Let's say a family of five counts as "extremely low income" as per above, so their income is around $29,000. The most they should be able to pay for housing each month and still "afford" it is about $700. ($700 x 12 monthly payments = $8,400, which is around 30 percent of $29,000.)

Another way to look at this is in terms of hourly wage. The National Low Income Housing Coalition issued a report in 2018, *Out of Reach*, which includes a chart explaining how much you would need to be paid hourly in order to afford an average two-bedroom apartment. In Hawaii, the most expensive state in the study, you would need to earn $36/hour! Put another way: at the minimum wage, you would need to work 143 hours a week (!) just to earn enough money for rent alone.

If these numbers hurt your brain, just consider the idea that there must be *some* threshold that makes housing too much of a burden. The more you pay for housing—which needs to include utilities, by the way—the less you have for groceries, clothes, and doctors' bills. And that is before you can even think about going to the movies, let alone taking a vacation. As the housing crisis intensifies, more and more people are finding it harder to get their housing costs to fall below that threshold or at least to not center their economic activity on paying their rent. As a result, advocates are moving past "homelessness" and "insecurity" to the term "**housing burden**" to talk about people who, although they may have a stable home for now, feel like they cannot truly afford where they live.

SO WHAT DO WE DO ABOUT IT?

As with many widespread social problems, housing is sometimes seen as an issue for chiefly the federal government to solve. Federal housing programs have certainly helped keep housing affordable for many: according to the Urban Institute, without federal housing programs *not one county in the country* would have enough housing for their neediest residents! Still, the solutions offered by the feds have been problematic at best. Subsidized "Section 8" vouchers have been somewhat successful: for people who qualify for the program, the government essentially pays their rent directly to their landlords. But funding for these vouchers has never kept up with demand, there are long waiting lists, and many landlords refuse to rent to qualified tenants due to the same fears about low-income citizens—again, unjustified!—noted above.

The other federal housing solution—public housing projects—was in vogue for decades after World War II, but has ended up concentrating the country's most impoverished residents in particular areas of cities. As I will discuss later in this book, the legacy of this kind of urban redevelopment is not the thriving local communities imagined by housing projects' original boosters. (In fact, the supposedly "blighted" communities bulldozed for these public housing projects were thriving minority communities.) Instead, the urban poor face a punishing bureaucracy that sees public housing residents as in need of policing, not support. And much of our public housing stock has been neglected for years, with very little being invested in maintenance and community programs. More and more, federal and local housing authorities are turning the projects over to private developers, who then convert the developments into mixed-income housing, decreasing the supply of affordable homes even further.

Public housing is often overseen by local governments, particularly local public housing authorities that are essentially special districts (remember those single-purpose governments from earlier!) that manage federal projects and funds. And as I noted when I introduced those special districts, housing authorities are key examples of how expertise requires a tradeoff with accountability. While some housing authorities are well run and work tirelessly to improve the lives of residents, many are badly in need of reform, operating without much public scrutiny whether they are managing properties or working to privatize them.

While we need to hold special districts to higher standards, there is much that general-purpose local governments can do as well. In fact, counties and cities have a number of important tools they can use to either promote the development of affordable housing—or make the problem worse.

First, local governments can **negotiate with developers** to increase the general supply of affordable housing. So a development company wants to buy or lease city land and build an apartment complex. Or a developer requires a change to local zoning laws in order to put up a mixed-use development of shops and homes. Fine, but the city or county can demand that the developer include a certain number or percentage of affordable units. The government cannot demand *too* much from the developer— a number of U.S. Supreme Court cases, most recently the 2013 *Koontz* decision, have established a required balance between developer rights and local government interests. But the Court has consistently recognized that local communities have legitimate interests in encouraging responsible development, and that they can use developer agreements to help address those interests.

Such negotiated requirements are commonly used but not always easy to enforce. Developers typically have more leverage. Local governments often are strapped for cash and desperately want the tax revenues from new buildings. If a developer does not like the strings attached to a project, they often have the resources to walk away from the deal and just wait for the next one. And even if the government succeeds in getting developers to agree to affordable unit requirements, that is only the first step. These requirements need teeth, including penalties if the developer/landlord reneges on the deal or slows down implementation ("Sorry, we just couldn't find enough low-income residents who qualify, and we tried really, *really* hard, I promise").

The solution that is most often reached in these negotiations is **"mixed-income" housing**. Developers make sure the majority of their homes are at market rates and combine them with a handful of income-qualifying affordable units. These kinds of developments are supposed to increase affordable housing stock without requiring expensive public subsidies—the profit from the market-rate homes essentially "pays for" lower-revenue units. But again, since these requirements effectively reduce developer profits, they are often difficult to negotiate and properly implement. Chicago, for example, has seen multiple problems with property managers imposing draconian rules on low-income renters, especially if they are mixed in with wealthier condominium owners. These rules are epitomized by the so-called "poor doors," or separate entrances for low-income renters as opposed to wealthier ones. Local governments need to demand and enforce the equal treatment of all residents regardless of income.

Local governments can make all this easier, some say, with another tool: the use of **inclusionary zoning**. County and city boards can build affordable housing requirements into local zoning regulations, so that there is no need to negotiate each time and developers know what to expect. Many of these regulations also build in incentives by offering density bonuses to developers, allowing them to build more units than would normally be legal if they include more affordable ones. Some localities even include options for the local government to buy affordable units at the end of a specified contract period, thus ensuring that they can maintain affordable housing stock.

Zoning laws do not have to concern themselves with only apartments—housing advocates suggest that local governments support different kinds of housing to increase density. For example, some localities have experimented with **accessory dwelling units (ADUs)**, sometimes called "granny flats." These are separate living spaces built on the same plot as single-family houses, and they range from basement or garage apartments to tiny houses. Although these kinds of dwellings address only a small fraction of the need for affordable housing, zoning rules and regulations can make these developments less expensive for homeowners and increase density in areas where new apartments are not as feasible.

Another useful tool that local governments can use is shared by the federal government: **tax incentives**. Since the 1980s, Congress has funded the Low-Income Housing Tax Credit program, which, administered through state housing agencies, gives developers a tax credit if they agree to rent a certain number of units at affordable rates. Local governments can and do offer similar tax abatements, giving landlords a break on property taxes in exchange for increasing affordable stock. Still, local governments need to pay attention to how these credits and incentives are used—those that are aimed at redeveloping "blighted" areas can end up accelerating the gentrification process, especially if left in place long after they are necessary. For example, in the mid-1990s, the city of Portland, Oregon, launched a prominent revitalization program in its "River District" using public dollars and including tax incentives that would require at least a third of new housing to be deemed affordable. The problem? The city found it difficult to keep track, and so basically just stopped counting. By the mid-2010s, over 90 percent of new construction in the area involved high-end developments, according to an analysis by *The Oregonian*.

While steady use of tax abatements can help build affordable housing stock, it can also get expensive for local governments. And so most housing advocates call for an additional tool: a **dedicated funding stream** from local government revenues. Most state governments have set up housing "trust funds" that invest in affordable housing through subsidies or grants, and that are typically funded by real estate transfer taxes. Local governments have also started developing similar funds. For example, in 2006 Virginia's Fairfax County established the "Penny Fund," which sets aside roughly one penny of each dollar of real estate tax revenue to fund affordable housing projects.

One other option for local governments is to establish a **community land bank**. This "bank" is actually a special-purpose government or district, sometimes contained within an economic development authority, which is granted ownership of trouble-some properties that local developers are afraid to touch. These properties are often, but do not necessarily have to be, in run-down areas of town; they can have delinquent taxes or title problems, or are just randomly abandoned and vacant. Land bank programs aim to return a property to private ownership, but the most successful land programs engage with the local commu-nity to help meet community needs—by adding a grocery store in a food desert, for example.

Local governments can also work with nonprofit groups, which often offer some ancillary support and solutions for addressing housing problems for citizens. A **community land trust**, for instance, is similar to a land bank, but instead of a government entity, a nonprofit owns a property while decisions about develop-ment are made by a community board. In some states, locals have negotiated **community benefit agreements**, in which developers promise to maintain wage floors and affordable housing targets in exchange for community support for their development projects. Local governments can make these types of arrangements easier or harder through legislation, regulation, or political support.

All of these varied solutions are really just scratching the surface of the problem of housing, which is complex and persistent. Still, it should be clear that you need at least a few factors in place to start to solve it. You need residents who are willing to overcome their (largely unfounded) fears about crime and property values. You need a government that prioritizes long-term development of housing density and diversity over immediate tax proceeds from sprawling single-family developments. And you need everyone to realize that a thriving locality needs people of all income levels to make it a nice place to live. A tall order, for sure, but a good community at least tries to make housing affordable and available to all.

SUMMARY

- <u>Affordable, stable housing</u> is an important need of local communities, providing <u>multiple economic and social benefits</u>.
- <u>Local housing authorities</u> maintain public housing projects, with mixed results.
- Economic trends, local laws, and cultural changes all contribute to a <u>crisis</u> in housing availability; unjustified <u>homeowner fears</u> and <u>short-sighted local leaders</u> do not help either.
- Local governments have a number of tools they can use to increase affordable housing stock, from <u>zoning laws</u> and <u>tax incentives</u> to <u>community land banks</u>.

ACTION STEPS

- *Support reform of local housing authorities.*
- *Support local laws that increase stock of affordable housing, from development incentives to inclusive zoning to community land banks.*
- *Support housing solutions from nonprofits, especially land trusts and banks.*
- *Help promote the idea of housing for all as an important right and social/economic need.*

WANT TO KNOW MORE?

For an overview of the problem of affordable housing, a good academic source is 2013's *Affordable Housing Reader*, which brings together classic and contemporary readings. If you want something less wonky, the Pulitzer Prize–winning *Evicted* by sociologist Matthew Desmond is not exactly about local politics, but it thoroughly humanizes the problem of housing and poverty. Many nonprofits offer data about the scope of the problem, such as the National Low Income Housing Coalition (www.nlihc.org) in their annual report *The Gap*.

For more on the numbers, Nuno Mota, an economist with Fannie Mae's Economic and Strategic Research Group, put together a "Housing Affordability Primer" in 2015 that is widely available online. A more academic perspective on the economics is featured in a 2004 paper by John M. Quigley and Steven Raphael in the *Journal of Economic Perspectives*.

Public housing has dominated public perception of low-income residents, with all sorts of resultant stigmas. As noted above, Fischel's book *Homevoter Hypothesis* explains the fears of homeowners and how they contribute to reducing the supply of housing. (As I suggested, Fischel is much more positive about the situation than others may be.) A more recent, well-regarded book on the problem of gentrification is Peter Moskowitz's *How to Kill a City*.

As for solutions, local governments and citizens interested in what might be possible—and what's legal—can check out *The Legal Guide to Affordable Housing Development*, written mostly by real estate attorneys. You can find the case for mixed-income housing, as well as the problems faced by Chicago officials in implementing this solution, in the 2015 book *Integrating the Inner City*. Community land trusts were first promoted by activist Robert Swann and his colleagues in the 1972 book *The Community Land Trust: A Guide to a New Model for Land Tenure in America*. Finally, in 2018 writer Benjamin Schneider published a succinct primer on inclusionary zoning on the indispensable *CityLab* website.

BIBLIOGRAPHY/FURTHER READING

Chaskin, Robert J., and Mark L. Joseph. 2015. *Integrating the Inner City: The Promise and Perils of Mixed-Income Public Housing Transformation*. Chicago: University of Chicago Press.

Desmond, Matthew. 2016. *Evicted: Poverty and Profit in the American City*. New York: Crown/Archetype.

Fischel, William A. 2009. *The Homevoter Hypothesis: How Home Values Influence Local Government Taxation, School Finance, and Land-Use Policies*. Cambridge, MA: Harvard University Press.

Getsinger, Liza, Katya Abazajian, Lily Posey, Graham MacDonald, and Josh Leopold. 2017. "The Housing Affordability Gap for Extremely Low income Renters in 2014." Washington, DC: Urban Institute.

Iglesias, Tim, and Rochelle E. Lento, eds. 2013. *The Legal Guide to Affordable Housing Development*. Second edition. Chicago: American Bar Association.

Metro Planning Council. 2018. "AMI and Housing Affordability." *Local Planning Handbook*. Saint Paul, MN: Metropolitan Council.

Moskowitz, P. E. 2017. *How to Kill a City: Gentrification, Inequality, and the Fight for the Neighborhood*. New York: Nation Books.

Mota, Nuno. 2015. "Housing Affordability Primer." New York: Fannie Mae.

National Low Income Housing Coalition. 2018. "Out of Reach: The High Cost of Housing." Washington, DC.

———. 2019. "The Gap: A Shortage of Affordable Homes." Washington, DC.

Quigley, John M., and Steven Raphael. 2004. "Is Housing Unaffordable? Why Isn't It More Affordable?" *Journal of Economic Perspectives* 18 (1): 191–214. https://doi.org/10.1257/089533004773563494.

Schneider, Benjamin. 2018. "CityLab University: Inclusionary Zoning." *CityLab*. July 17. https://www.citylab.com/equity/2018/07/citylab-university-inclusionary-zoning/565181/.

Swann, Robert, Shimon Gottschalk, Erick S. Hansch, and Edward Webster. 1972. *The Community Land Trust: A Guide to a New Model for Land Tenure in America*. Cambridge, MA: Center for Community Economic Development.

Tighe, Rosie, and Elizabeth Mueller. 2013. *The Affordable Housing Reader*. New York: Routledge.

SUPPORT PUBLIC TRANSIT

We are all probably familiar with the version of the American dream often promoted in the years after World War II. As noted in the last chapter, the suburban, "Leave It to Beaver" America of the 1950s promised everyone their own home, with a white picket fence and a car in the driveway. Yet this suburban vision was a contrast to where people actually lived. Immediately following the war, you could in fact find most Americans in cities. In 1950, the ten largest cities in the country were home to one out of every six Americans.

However, this changed dramatically over the next few decades. A series of national and local policies almost literally drove people away from cities. By the year 2000, those ten central cities were home to only one out of every fourteen Americans.

Today, Americans are mostly spread out. But we are not so sure that we like it.

Recent generations are becoming more and more interested in city and town centers where they can walk, bike, and scooter around without having to drive long distances or fight for parking. Young people seem to want "dense" and "mixed-use" development allowing them to shop, work, and live in the same, relatively small area. Their desires are in part driven by a stronger environmental consciousness than that of previous generations, including concern for minimizing their carbon footprint. But maybe these folks have also grown up with their parents' long commutes and dispersed communities and have recognized that a life with urban-style density is often just plain better.

One significant feature that these younger folks increasingly support and that makes a walkable, dense community possible is **public transit**. Transit options are popular: a 2015 report from the Mineta Transportation Institute showed that a consistent and strong majority of Americans saw the benefits of public transit to their communities and supported improving transit when possible. (There was much less support for *paying* for those improvements, but we will get to that.)

Unfortunately, public transit has not always been the most popular idea in local politics in the past. In fact, the decades-long history of suburban American ideals has continued to undermine the development of transit options to the point where we now often look down on those who take the bus. How did we get here?

WHAT HAPPENED? A SHORT HISTORY

It is widely accepted by observers that public transit in America is in pretty bad shape, certainly in comparison with other developed countries. Effective high-speed rail runs all across Europe, and many cities in Asia have highly developed transit systems. Not so in America: according to the nonprofit American Public Transit Association, 45 percent of Americans have no access to public transit of any kind.

It wasn't always like this. In the first third of the twentieth century, most urban workers commuted to work on extensive streetcar systems, mostly run by thriving private conglomerates.

Cities like New York and Chicago had invested in railway networks, both above- and underground. And yet, today, only 5 percent of commuters use public transit and almost three-quarters of Americans get to work by driving alone.

What happened?

Streetcar systems died, of course. A popular conspiracy theory has, for decades, suggested that the country's major car companies bought up streetcar operators to put them out of business. But although corporations like GM and Standard Oil did purchase a lot of these streetcar concerns, their motivation was much simpler: they wanted to monopolize the sales of tires, fuel, and equipment as the streetcars were converted into buses. (In a 1947 federal court case, the car companies were even convicted of these monopolistic sales practices, but not of a conspiracy to destroy streetcars.)

In fact, the death of streetcars had started earlier, during the Great Depression, when rising prices and declining ridership caused some streetcar companies to go out of business. Even after the economic recovery, streetcars found themselves behind schedule as newly popular private autos clogged the streets—and damaged the same roads that streetcar companies had foolishly promised to be responsible for maintaining. Many streetcar companies had also agreed to stringent price controls and could not raise their fares to cover the new costs; they cut service instead, driving down ridership. Most of the surviving companies eventually converted to buses just to try to stay in business. So a combination of economic forces and misguided choices led to the death of the streetcar.

Similarly unwise choices by government officials also made things much worse for public transit after World War II. The federal government invested in a huge project that completely undermined public transit: the **Interstate Highway System**, spurred famously in part by Eisenhower's vision of a national roadway system as a necessary component of homeland security and defense. Infrastructure dollars were spread across the country, with hundreds of billions going to developing highways, bridges, and tunnels. Roads were wonderful for rural areas, but in cities they were often directed through existing neighborhoods, devastating and displacing low-income communities. These often thriving neighborhoods—typically the homes of blacks and other minorities—were universally dismissed as "blighted" and needing "renewal." (I will discuss urban renewal in more detail later in the book.)

These downtown highways were supposed to support city business districts, providing workers from nearby suburbs with an easy way to commute to urban jobs. But they also enabled the departure of this entire workforce from within urban borders, hastening the sprawling growth of suburbia and draining city tax rolls of their middle-class and wealthy citizens. Businesses and jobs eventually followed, especially as technological advances made it easier to decentralize manufacturing and services. And so it is no exaggeration to say that federal dollars essentially flowed through the states to encourage them to push everyone into cars and to hollow out their cities. Almost everyone who could afford it bought a car and moved away, leaving behind the urban poor to make do with whatever transit services were left.

Roads by themselves may not have signaled the death of public transit. But unlike our European counterparts, American cities did not continue to invest in rail and bus systems alongside the growth of highways, even in places with well-developed subway systems like New York City. And whereas the size and scope of our country certainly present more challenges in terms of transportation than the smaller countries of Europe, our Canadian neighbors have managed to accommodate the sprawl of their cities while still building out successful transit systems.

The eventual result is what we are faced with today: an aging, underdeveloped transit network that is widely perceived to be part of the social safety net. In other words, to many citizens and officials, public transit is not a vital government service for everyone in a locality but rather government aid for the poor. Although this approach encourages localities to subsidize service and keep fares affordable, it also undermines investment and expansion. Transit becomes just another social welfare program competing for limited funding from cash-strapped cities and counties.

Some fans of public transit, therefore, were excited by the recent entrance into the transit market of ridesharing and other "disruptive" models from private companies. But "micro-transit" corporations like Chariot and Bridj that have tried to match users with vanpools have so far proven unsuccessful as anything but a niche program, possibly replacing public paratransit systems that offer subsidized rides to people with disabilities or seniors. And whereas rideshare companies like Uber and Lyft have proven popular with urban residents, they remain heavily subsidized. Although these companies often publicly tout their role as a complement to public transit, Uber's IPO documentation baldly noted how the company actually saw public transit systems as a competitor that it sought to undermine and possibly replace.

Many public transit advocates now call for increased federal investment in transportation infrastructure. But they often find a national government uninterested in the problems of concentrated populations. Thanks to the structure of our federal government, urban interests are underrepresented despite the fact that only one in five Americans still lives in a rural area. Because of the constitutional compromise that grants small states the same number of senators as large states, and because this compromise affects the Electoral College, outsized electoral influence is given to smaller populations in rural areas. Other rules, like federal programs that guarantee a minimum of aid to each state, also over-reward smaller, rural populations. Local governments, particularly urban ones, often end up on their own.

BENEFITS OF PUBLIC TRANSIT

What makes this history of neglect especially troubling is that the benefits of public transit are pretty widely accepted by scholars and experts, though not always as well recognized by America's car-loving public. In fact, there are three main areas where public transit can make a difference: **lower levels of pollution**, **reduced traffic congestion**, and **economic development**. I'll run through each of these below.

Lower Levels of Pollution

According to the U.S. Environmental Protection Agency, almost a third of the country's greenhouse gas emissions are produced by transportation, with almost two-thirds of that fraction generated by "light-duty vehicles," i.e. you in your car. Public transit systems show immense potential for reducing those emissions. I say "potential" because the actual data shows that public transit has so far not reduced pollution by as much as some advocates would hope.

A 2017 "programmatic assessment" by the Federal Transit Administration argued that the addition of more transit options to a city's network did reduce emissions, but not by as much as originally estimated when taking into account the pollution generated by construction. Other research suggests that investments in hybrid vehicles and High-Occupancy Vehicle (HOV) lanes may reduce pollution by as much as public transit. Unfortunately, the math is hard and there is not a lot of data available. Localities are hopeful, though, that such investments can make an immediate difference. A number of cities outside of the U.S., from Paris to Seoul, have offered free public transit during smog emergencies, for example, although with uncertain results.

Because of the complicated scale of environmental problems, investments in large-scale public transit projects, like additional subway lines or light rail, have uncertain effects on environmental pollution. These kinds of projects require expensive construction (which, again, generates emissions of its own) and may take years, if not decades, to reward localities. For example, the city of Toronto added the Sheppard Line to its subway system in 2002; a 2017 study suggested that the emissions "payback" may take as long as thirty-five years.

Still, the general consensus among urban planners and scholars is that public transit probably makes a difference in terms of pollution, especially if transit efforts are combined with development policies that move toward greater population density and an integrated network of jobs and homes. In other words, public transit options will not help the environment much if everyone still takes buses and trains miles and miles to work each day. By itself, this spotty data record of environmental progress may not be enough to justify the high cost of transit improvements. Luckily, there are other benefits to add to the list.

Reduced Traffic Congestion

Economists and traffic experts have argued for decades that the solution to congested highways is *not* the most obvious one—more highways. Economist and public policy scholar Anthony Downs pointed out the "law of peak-hour traffic congestion" as far back as 1962: as Downs noted, traffic will increase during peak hours to the maximum capacity of the roads. What he is describing here can be captured by a key term from economics: **induced demand**. This concept suggests that the more of something there is, the more people will consume it, so the creation of more stuff *induces* or encourages people to use that stuff. Lots of studies on highway congestion suggest that induced demand is a core driver of highway use. So if a city or state is suffering from traffic, building additional highway capacity may just add more cars to the roads and not help the problem at all.

So is public transit the answer to congested highways? Some think so, but the issue is again complicated by mixed results and a lack of clear data. Some folks, largely from libertarian sources, disagree with this line of thinking. They argue that induced demand is often confused with "latent" demand—users who want to use the roads but currently cannot as opposed to users who are essentially generated, or lured in, by the new construction. And even the studies that argue that induced demand is a problem in the case of car usage do not necessarily conclude that improved public transit would create the same kind of pressure on demand—building more public transit might not automatically cause more people to switch to trains and buses.

Anthony Downs is again important here, as he also argued—as did economist J. M. Thomson—that investing in highways can essentially starve public transport, leaving users of both transit and highways worse off. If you keep building roads instead of bus or rail lines, induced demand could encourage people to continue to use roads at maximum capacity, but the resulting disinvestment of public transit would lead to a downward spiral of reduced service and lowered ridership. This "Downs–Thomson paradox"—that essentially more roads screw *everybody* up—has been supported quite a bit by the transportation literature.

One additional factor related to congestion, which does not often get discussed, is **traffic injuries and fatalities**. We often act as if people getting hit by cars is just a fact of modern life. But if you reduce traffic and the number of cars on the road, you almost automatically reduce the number of traffic accidents, injuries, and—most importantly—deaths. Recognizing this, "Vision Zero" is an international program designed to rally a locality's citizens and policymakers around the idea that traffic deaths are preventable, not inevitable. First developed in Sweden and since adopted by a number of American cities, it encourages local governments to reshape laws, roads, and traffic patterns using a systematic approach designed to reduce or even eliminate deaths from traffic accidents. Groups like the Vision Zero Network and the American Public Transit Association have argued that public transit must be a core component of these zero-death approaches: cities with significant public transportation options have much lower traffic fatality rates than the rest of the country.

Economic Development

So far we may have found only a lukewarm case for public transit. But economic development is where you really get the most bang for your buck out of bus and rail systems. Robust public transportation options help keep an economy humming.

Another fancy economic term is **economies of agglomeration**. This last word may sound like a supervillain, but it just means that when people are packed together—or "agglomerated"—in dense urban settlements, a number of economic benefits follow. This is largely because it helps when economic activity is concentrated. Suppliers are close to production facilities. Workers live near their jobs. Employers have plenty of choices of people to hire and lots of customers for their services and products. All the benefits of "network effects" and "economies of scale" (sorry, more economic terms) that come from concentrated economic activity are found in dense city centers.

And robust public transportation options can be a central contributor to these economic effects. A 2013 study by two urban planning scholars argued that a strong public transportation network can contribute billions in economic activity due to these agglomeration effects. If more local government officials took these effects into account, these planners argued, they would see that investments in public transport pay off more forcefully and quickly.

On the flip side, a lack of investment in public transit systems can be very costly for businesses. A 2018 report from the American Public Transit Association looked at cities with existing transit systems and argued that a failure to invest in and modernize rail and bus lines would lead to millions, if not billions, in lost revenue for local businesses. A transit system characterized by delays and breakdowns can lead to a city and economy plagued by lower production and lost wages, as well as a lack of access to jobs.

One thing liberals and conservatives often agree on is: **infrastructure spending** is good for the economy. In fact, we have decades of research that suggests that this kind of spending—maintaining roads, highways, and bridges, strengthening public utilities like gas and water, and also funding public transit systems—adds jobs and boosts wages, while producing significant impacts on local economies. Some more conservative and libertarian types worry about throwing money at infrastructure without careful planning, but even these folks recognize that locally driven, necessary investments in infrastructure maintenance and development, including transit, spur economic growth.

Transit development may also have a positive effect on surrounding property values. There is growing evidence that a **"transit premium"** may apply to commercial and residential real estate near transportation hubs like bus and train stations. This effect depends on a bunch of factors, including walkability, access to jobs, and maturity of the transit system—a brand new bus stop in a low-income neighborhood with no local businesses may not have much of an immediate effect. Still, Americans unsurprisingly want to live near employment opportunities, and as I noted at the beginning of this chapter, walkable "mixed-use" developments are increasingly favored by young professionals. Public transit can be a key part of that lifestyle.

A warning may be useful here: some of these economic benefits may be overstated. As I noted earlier in this book, analysts love to issue reports with wild claims of billions of dollars in economic impact. But when you combine all of the different arguments and evidence—property values, network effects, agglomeration, economies of scale, infrastructure spending, economic efficiency—it becomes difficult to deny that public transit helps a local economy grow.

Of course, we could also draw a moral corollary from all of these economic arguments for transit investment. For many low-income workers, public transportation is their *only* option for getting to a job; their local bus stop may literally be their one path to economic opportunity. Local governments owe it to these folks to make sure they can earn a living to support themselves and their families. This is true not just because such access is an important contributor to the economic health of a locality, although it most certainly is, but also because it is the right thing to do.

SOLUTIONS

Beyond a wide-scale transformation in American priorities, what can local governments and citizens do to expand and support public transit? Again, young folks are often choosing more sustainable lifestyles: they move to urban areas with high population density, walkability, and bikeability, and—when given the option—public transportation. Still, these are mobile professionals, and it is not clear how long they even stay in such areas. As they age and their families grow, they may buy into the older American dream of a two-car garage in the suburbs. So what else can we do?

Advocacy is, of course, of vital importance. Many localities have local nonprofits that work with their governments and transit authorities to push for more funding, transparency, and equity. For example, Atlanta's MARTA system is watchdogged by Citizens for Progressive Transit and more recently, the "MARTA Army." National umbrella groups like the American Public Transit Association and the National Alliance of Public Transportation Advocates try to network these efforts and support advocacy all across the country.

At the local level, we can choose solutions that try to develop public transit options without breaking the bank. Most localities are not going to invest in building a new train system, for example, due to the huge amount of time and money needed. But many advocates are turning toward high-speed, dedicated bus lines—**BRT, or Bus Rapid Transit**, is less costly, more flexible, and with natural gas fuels, often better for the environment than other forms of infrastructure development. Other localities are experimenting with vanpools and park-and-rides. But overall, more service is key: if you offer a convenient and affordable option for even middle-class commuters, they will often find that it is better to abandon their cars.

On a related note, transportation advocates argue that more frequent service, spread out over widely dispersed stops and stations, would be more appealing to middle-class commuters and would build usage and support for the system overall. This could be a good thing for transit systems desperate for more attention and support, but there is one problem: more frequency often translates into less coverage, meaning some areas that desperately need service may not get it. And although transit is not *just* for the poor, the fact remains that many low-income people rely on transit because it is their *only* option. Sure, you want to expand the use of bus and rail options, but your city or county cannot abandon the people who need public transportation the most. Better service and wider benefits cannot come at the cost of hurting your locality's most vulnerable residents.

So with public transit, as always, the choices we make at the local and state levels matter. We need more frequency *and* more coverage. Maintaining roads is of course an important goal for all levels of government, but before investing in widening lanes and highways, we should direct public dollars to transit alternatives whenever possible. All of this requires money—local, state, and even federal money, if we can get it. It may be hard, but it is necessary; the benefits of public transit are clear.

SUMMARY

- More and more, people want to live in areas with reliable, frequent <u>public transit</u> options.
- Local, state, and federal governments have <u>underinvested</u> in public transit for years, the result being that transit is seen as only a <u>welfare benefit</u>, not a <u>necessary public service</u>.
- Public transit has multiple benefits for localities, including <u>reduced pollution</u>, <u>reduced traffic congestion and fatalities</u>, and especially <u>increased economic opportunities</u>.

ACTION STEPS

- *Support investment in public transit.*
- *Support transit plans and systems that balance more frequency (to attract middle-class commuters) and more coverage (to ensure equal access to the system).*

WANT TO KNOW MORE?

For a general overview of transit, Jarrett Walker's blog (www.humantransit.org) and 2013 book *Human Transit* are good places to start. If you want to read more about the history of streetcars and disinvestment, science journalist Joseph Stromberg did a remarkable series of articles for *Vox* in 2015–16. For urban renewal and federal highways specifically, you could look at James Q. Wilson's classic book *Urban Renewal*, or more recently, Samuel Zipp's *Manhattan Projects*, which is about New York City in particular. The *CityLab* website also reports regularly on the history and current state of public transit.

The federal government's data on emissions is captured in the EPA's annual *Inventory of U.S. Greenhouse Gas Emissions and Sinks* (available on its website at https://www.epa.gov/ghgemissions/inventory-us-greenhouse-gas-emissions-and-sinks).

Anthony Downs's 1992 book *Stuck in Traffic: Coping with Peak-Hour Traffic Congestion* sums up much of his research on induced demand, traffic congestion, and the public transport paradox; a revised edition, *Still Stuck in Traffic*, was released in 2005. If you want to read a more scholarly economics paper (although if you do, maybe see a therapist), many people cite a 2011 study by economists Gilles Duranton and Matthew Turner. A similar paper in *Urban Studies* in 2013 connects public transit to agglomeration effects.

The Vision Zero Network lays out the "Vision Zero" approach to eliminating traffic fatalities on its website (visionzeronetwork. org). The American Public Transport Association (APTA) offers lots of related research and information, including a 2018 report on public transit and Vision Zero ("Public Transit Is Key Strategy in Advancing Vision Zero, Eliminating Traffic Fatalities"). APTA also worked with the National Association of Realtors to commission a study on the effects of public transport on property values ("The New Real Estate Mantra: Location near Public Transportation").

One of the many examples to demonstrate the case for infrastructure spending can be found in a 2019 report from the liberal Center on Budget and Policy Priorities titled "It's Time for States to Invest in Infrastructure." As for the other side of the political spectrum, Jim Manzi laid out the conservative case for infrastructure in a widely read article in the conservative journal *National Affairs* ("The New American System" in spring 2014). Ryan Bourne of the libertarian Cato Institute offered more measured support for infrastructure investments in a 2017 policy

brief ("Would More Government Infrastructure Spending Boost
the U.S. Economy?"), still seeing the benefits of maintaining
local control.

BIBLIOGRAPHY/FURTHER READING

Agrawal, Asha Weinstein. 2015. "What Do Americans Think about
Public Transit? A Review of U.S. Public Opinion Polling Survey
Questions." San Jose, CA: Mineta Transportation Institute.

Becker, Sofia, Scott Bernstein, and Linda Young. 2013. "The New Real
Estate Mantra: Location Near Public Transportation." Washington,
DC: American Public Transportation Association and National
Association of Realtors.

Bourne, Ryan. 2017. "Would More Government Infrastructure Spending
Boost the U.S. Economy?" Cato Institute. June 6. https://www.
cato.org/publications/policy-analysis/would-more-government-
infrastructure-spending-boost-us-economy.

Chatman, Daniel G., and Robert B. Noland. 2014. "Transit
Service, Physical Agglomeration and Productivity in US
Metropolitan Areas." *Urban Studies* 51 (5): 917–37. https://doi.
org/10.1177/0042098013494426.

Dickens, Matthew, and Leah Shaum. 2018. "Public Transit Is Key
Strategy in Advancing Vision Zero, Eliminating Traffic Fatalities."
Washington, DC: American Public Transportation Association.

Downs, Anthony. 1992. "The Law of Peak-Hour Highway Congestion."
Traffic Quarterly 16 (3): 393–409.

———. 2005. *Still Stuck in Traffic: Coping with Peak-Hour Traffic
Congestion*. Washington, DC: Brookings Institution Press.

Duranton, Gilles, and Matthew A. Turner. 2011. "The Fundamental Law
of Road Congestion: Evidence from US Cities." *American Economic
Review* 101 (6): 2616–2652. https://doi.org/10.1257/aer.101.6.2616.

Filosa, Gina, Carson Poe, and Maya Sarna. 2017. "Greenhouse Gas
Emissions from Transit Projects: Programmatic Assessment."
Washington, DC: Federal Transit Administration. https://rosap.ntl.
bts.gov/view/dot/12407.

Gordon, Aaron. 2019. "Uber (Finally) Admits It's Directly Competing with Public Transportation." *Jalopnik*. April 12. https://jalopnik.com/uber-finally-admits-its-directly-competing-with-publi-1834009027.

Manzi, Jim. 2014. "The New American System." *National Affairs*. Spring. https://www.nationalaffairs.com/publications/detail/the-new-american-system.

McNichol, Elizabeth. 2016. "It's Time for States to Invest in Infrastructure." Washington, DC: Center on Budget and Policy Priorities. https://www.cbpp.org/research/state-budget-and-tax/its-time-for-states-to-invest-in-infrastructure.

Saxe, Shoshanna, Eric Miller, and Eric Guthrie. 2017. "The Net Greenhouse Gas Impact of the Sheppard Subway Line." *Transportation Research Part D: Transport and Environment* 51 (March): 261–75.

Stromberg, Joseph. 2015a. "The Real Story behind the Demise of America's Once-Mighty Streetcars." *Vox*. May 7. https://www.vox.com/2015/5/7/8562007/streetcar-history-demise.

———. 2015b. "Highways Gutted American Cities. So Why Did They Build Them?" *Vox*. May 14. https://www.vox.com/2015/5/14/8605917/highways-interstate-cities-history.

———. 2015c. "The Real Reason American Public Transportation Is Such a Disaster." *Vox*. August 10. https://www.vox.com/2015/8/10/9118199/public-transportation-subway-buses.

Walker, Jarrett. 2012. *Human Transit: How Clearer Thinking about Public Transit Can Enrich Our Communities and Our Lives*. Washington, DC: Island Press.

Wilson, James Q. 1966. *Urban Renewal: The Record and the Controversy*. Cambridge, MA: MIT Press.

Zipp, Samuel. 2010. *Manhattan Projects: The Rise and Fall of Urban Renewal in Cold War New York*. New York: Oxford University Press.

SAY "YES" TO REGIONAL COOPERATION

In September of 2017, the giant online retailer Amazon announced that it was looking to establish a second corporate headquarters to supplement its existing Seattle location. This "HQ2" announcement spurred a frenzy of competition, with over 200 proposals submitted from state and local governments vying for the company's projected $5-billion construction investment and 50,000 jobs. Some observers wondered whether local governments might be offering too generous incentive packages in a desperate attempt to outdo each other; the eventual winner might have given up so much that they would end up losing in the deal. *Saturday Night Live* even produced a sketch in which city delegations plied Amazon CEO Jeff Bezos with freebies such as local beverages, dishes, and even pop stars. ("Today we give you . . . a souvenir of our city: Pitbull!")

But this public free-for-all was not an isolated incident. The battle for HQ2 was just the most recent manifestation of a long-term competition local governments are engaged in. Thanks to some built-in features of local government in the U.S., cities, towns, and counties are all subject to economic pressures that pit them against each other. Like lone wolves in the winter fighting over the same scraps of food, local governments are forced to compete for scarce economic development dollars. And just like with Amazon, even the winning local governments, and especially their most vulnerable citizens, often end up losing instead.

The way to make sure everyone wins may seem obvious: local governments should work together, not against each other. But with strong incentives against cooperation, working together is actually much harder than it sounds. Still, despite the challenges, cooperation among geographically close local governments— **regional cooperation**, or **regionalism**—may be the only way out of this economic battle.

To understand the promise and challenges of regional cooperation, a little background is necessary. Below, I will show how some longstanding arguments in the study of local government helped social scientists frame our understanding of this problem, and why some of these same social scientists think regionalism is such a promising solution. (There is a lot of theory here, but don't worry too much—there are cupcakes, too.) By the end of this chapter, you should understand why your city or county often seems to cut bad deals—and more importantly, what they should do differently next time.

LOCAL INTERESTS

As with many other things in America, the study of social science flourished after World War II. While the economy boomed and the country developed a national infrastructure, scholars turned their attention to the development of modern democratic practices and the general role of power in society. They basically asked, "Who's in charge here?" And in part because scientists had not yet developed the tools for regularly conducting surveys and analyses on a national scale, they focused on the same thing I focus on in this book: local communities.

The ensuing "community power debate" examined how governance works at the local level; it also framed how social scientists would understand power and democracy over the next few decades and really set the agenda for many studies in politics. The debate spawned a number of important theories that we still discuss today in political science classes and scholarly journals. It clarified our understanding of power and how it works. And, for better or for worse, the debate forced scholars to take sides.

In fact, there were two prominent arguments that developed out of this study of democracy in local communities. The first argument resulted from different answers to that question of who is in charge. One group of scholars led by a University of North Carolina sociologist named Floyd Hunter argued that a group made up of mostly business elites effectively decides what happens in a local community. Hunter had kicked off the entire debate with his influential 1953 book *Community Power Structure*, which used a then-novel "reputational" method to identify the people with power in the city of Atlanta. Fellow sociologist C. Wright Mills would later take this line of thinking further and argue that a "**power elite**" of business, political, and military leaders essentially runs the country with very little democratic input. (This idea is actually way less paranoid than it sounds.)

These "power elite" sociologists were challenged a decade later by Yale political scientist Robert Dahl, who conducted his own study of a city—his home of New Haven, Connecticut. In *Who Governs?*, Dahl proposed the influential theory of **pluralism**, suggesting that power is instead distributed among different groups and negotiated through the political process. Although Dahl admitted that not everyone participates in politics—lack of wealth and other inequalities make it hard for some to break into the political "stratum" or arena—no single group is able to dominate the political process. For Dahl and his pluralist pals, government is therefore more responsive to the people than the "elite" sociologists would allow.

A lot of scholars took up one side or the other in this debate. Most of the political scientists relied on some version of pluralism to inform their studies of local or national democracy, while it was mostly sociologists, particularly the more radical scholars of the 1960s and 1970s, who followed Mills and Hunter in pointing to the influence of elites. But both of these sides eventually became joined, at least in studies of local politics, in opposition to a new set of claims about governance. This second major debate is probably best characterized as a choice between **structure** and **agency**.

Even though they offered different answers, both the pluralists and the "power elite" theorists shared that one big question, "Who's in charge here?" They focused on human *agency*—the idea that the way to understand how local government (and government in general) works is to look at the *people* involved. But a number of scholars wanted to answer the question in a different way. What if the answer to "Who's in charge here?" were "no one"? What if politics were shaped not by people, but mostly by impersonal forces?

This new group countered the power of agency with the power of *structure*. They argued that socioeconomic forces, particularly economic power and pressure, are a more important influence on politics and policymaking than whatever person or group effectively runs a locality. A lot of the pro-structure scholars were influenced by Marxism, which was not that outlandish for a generation formed by the 1960s. But you did not need to buy into Marx's ideas to recognize that economic forces shape the choices of local governments no matter who is in charge.

The most powerful version of this argument appeared when Harvard political scientist Paul Peterson published *City Limits* in

1981. Although he was no Marxist, Peterson clearly was on the "structure" side of the local politics debate. And he combined his structuralist concerns with another idea he got from a couple of other scholars, particularly his Harvard colleague Edward Banfield—that local governments have **interests**.

This may sound dumb, or weird. We probably intuitively get the idea that *people* have interests; it is in my long-term interest not to eat too much ice cream, for example, while my short-term interest may be aimed at grabbing that milkshake after lunch. But it can be useful to think about the interests of a particular locality or government, too. International politics scholars talk about interests in this way all the time; they often ask, for instance, whether or not a military, diplomatic, or trade policy is in a country's interest. Peterson explained the local version of this idea using the example of a public school system. Within schools, teachers, principals, and students may all have different interests because of their different roles in the system. But getting more financial aid from the state or winning the state basketball tournament would provide overall benefits that help everyone, and so these events are in the interest of the school system as a whole.

So what is in a city's or a county's interest? Peterson identified three things that any local government wants to maintain or improve. The first is *political power*, because—maybe obviously—having more room to operate in the political arena makes it easier to get what you want. Second is *social prestige*, because a "cool" city or "hot" county can more easily attract residents and businesses. The third, at least according to Peterson, is what dominates local governance: **economic position**. Whether or not they are right, cities and other local governments seem to think that the area they can most affect is economic standing, and so most of their efforts go toward improving the local economy.

But in working to improve their economies, local governments are aiming for a particular *type* of economy: an "export model." If bakers in Cupcake County produce a particularly excellent variety of baked goods, they will be able to sell and ship these goods to other nearby localities, and then maybe even to places beyond. To produce their cakes, they need to hire more workers, possibly even luring them in from outside the county. Bakers may need more and more products and services from other local industries—sugar and butter from local suppliers, baking websites from IT workers, even rope courses and escape rooms to build camaraderie among their employees. The bakers' well-paid employees will rent fancy lofts in town centers and spend their salaries at local restaurants, helping to put more money in the pockets of workers in other industries. The fuel for this economic boom is more than just the domestic trade from "taking in one another's laundry," in Peterson's words; instead, it is fed by money coming in from outside the county for those sweet, sweet cupcakes.

All of this may sound great (unless you're on a diet): a booming cupcake industry where the local economy thrives. But Peterson recognized a serious problem for counties like the hypothetical Cupcake County: what if nearby Sugar County does a better job of luring in bakers? Or even Flour City in the next state over? "Export" industries, particularly in today's global economy, are fairly *mobile*: many companies have a lot of options of where to settle. What if your county or city ends up having to compete for a company's favor, as in the Amazon HQ2 example that opened this chapter? How far will your local government go to land that company? And what happens if it—and you—lose?

RACE TO THE BOTTOM

Peterson's book identified a few of the resources local governments have at their disposal to recruit this kind of capital investment from export industries like the cupcake bakers. Cities can offer financial concessions, for example by exempting a relocating company from certain taxes or fees. Or a county can offer favorable utility rates—free water or low-cost gas may lure in a manufacturing plant. The crucial resource local governments can control, though, is *land*.

Some localities are blessed with advantages over others such as access to water routes, transportation, even climate and natural beauty. (People are more likely to vacation in Florida than in the Dakotas.) But all localities have to be smart about *how* they use their geographic features. All the natural beauty in the world will not matter if your zoning laws allow manufacturing concerns to poison your county's air and water; connection to a passenger train artery may not help your city if you don't invest internally in local transit.

This is again why, as I keep pointing out, *the* issue for local governments is land use and development. (As Peterson wrote in his book, "Urban politics is above all the politics of land use.") Cities, counties, and towns can and do use whatever land rules they have—including zoning laws, building regulations, and eminent domain or the ability to seize private land for public use—to create favorable conditions for export industries to choose to locate within their borders.

But all of these pressures create a peculiar dynamic for local governments, with two huge negative consequences. First, cities and counties want to attract capital investment, but they also want to attract the labor to support this capital—workers, in other words. But not all workers are equal; most localities end up competing for the highly skilled, white-collar workers who typically support export industries. These are trained technicians of various kinds, plus a professional and managerial class: think the IT guy, plus his mid-level manager, her CEO, and her CEO's attorney. Since any lower-skilled jobs are much easier to fill than these positions, local governments do not want to attract too many "unemployables," who are not as sought after and—if they fail to get a job—may require support from social services.

If this sounds like it could get ugly, that is because it often does. Cities, counties, and towns are essentially led by these structural economic pressures into class warfare. Local governments want to invest in services and amenities for the middle class so they can attract "good" labor without companies having to pay too high wages, but they are less likely to invest in important social services that are needed by lower-income citizens and that the middle class typically does not use. So smart counties try to maintain excellent parks, recreation, and school systems. Cities develop thriving arts and culture districts, with fancy museums and music venues. But all of these governments are less inclined to create free health clinics or homeless shelters beyond the bare minimum to keep the streets free of bodies to step over.

This kind of policymaking contributes to wealth concentration and economic segregation—and, thanks to the longstanding demographics of inequality in our country, racial segregation as well. Lower-income families have to go *somewhere*, and whichever neighborhood they are pushed into is not typically a thriving one. As I noted elsewhere, this kind of segregated living was boosted for decades by federal government policies that supported highways over public transit and concentrated the poor in federal housing projects. All of this is obviously bad for vulnerable populations, but it is not even that wonderful for the middle class either. Many of the even high-skilled workers prized by localities essentially have been pushed out of urban centers into overdeveloped suburbs filled with strip malls and big box stores, with poor air quality and long commutes.

The other negative consequence of structural pressures on localities is that economic development becomes at its heart a high-stakes competition. And this battle pits city against city, county against county, and sometimes city against surrounding counties, in a zero-sum war for companies' favor. If an auto plant locates in your county, that is a gain for you and bad news for my city—a loss of potential tax revenue and jobs for my residents. This loss is more literal if the plant was originally located in my city. This dynamic gives tons of leverage to companies looking to relocate, or at least threatening to do so. Which city or county can offer the best package of tax giveaways and favorable utility rates? Which locality can promise to offer the best amenities for middle- and upper-class workers without "wasting" money on services for the poor?

The result is often a ruthless competition, a "race to the bottom" in which each local government tries to do the best job of screwing the poor and/or giving up more revenue in tax abatements than they might bring in from economic development. You end up with the state of Texas placing radio ads in California that offer lower taxes and less regulation to literally lure businesses away. On the flip side, you get cities like San Francisco giving homeless residents bus tickets to Indianapolis, as *The Guardian* reported in 2017. And based on the arguments of Peterson and other structuralists like him, cities and counties basically have *no choice* in the matter—economic conditions dictate this kind of competition as the smart play. And there is nothing anyone can do about it.

Or is there?

HOW TO FIX IT

To be sure, not every social scientist has agreed with the structuralists; one dissenter is a prominent New York City policy scholar named John Mollenkopf. He argued that although Peterson and his friends were right to emphasize economic constraints on local governments, we should not therefore be economic "determinists." Politics still matters, Mollenkopf wrote, and local officials and political coalitions can deal with the structural problems Peterson outlined in many different ways. For example, any city may come to see that investing in public transport is one way to become more attractive for capital investment. But *how* that city invests—rail versus bus, connections to poor neighborhoods versus wealthy suburbs, etc.—can affect different communities in various ways.

Mollenkopf joined with two other well-known scholars of urban politics, Peter Dreier and Todd Swanstrom, to write the award-winning 2001 book *Place Matters*. (The third edition was released in 2014, just to give you an idea of the book's impact.) The three progressive scholars addressed the problems of local governance, particularly economic segregation and inequality, and proposed a number of solutions. Though they acknowledged the kinds of constraints on localities that Peterson proposed, these authors felt that there are ways that local government leaders can deal with them.

Place Matters suggests two types of solution in particular. The first requires government action at the national level. The federal government is not subject to the same economic constraints as local governments: national borders are more strongly enforced than local ones, and the feds can borrow money and go into debt much more easily. So services for low-income communities should be a national concern, the book argues. (Some observers have noted that in Europe, where the welfare safety net is much more robust than in the U.S., local government competition seems much less pronounced.)

But change from the feds is outside the scope of this book; we are much more concerned here with the second answer, which details what to do at the local level. *Place Matters* argues that local governments can approach the problems of competition head-on and defuse them by cooperating instead of competing with each other. This "new regionalism" that started spreading in the 1990s, the authors knew, would not completely eliminate the structural constraints facing cities and counties. However, **regional cooperation** could help blunt the force of these pressures and give local governments some room to maneuver in ways that could really help their citizens.

There are many ways that local governments in a particular region can cooperate. In most cases, representatives from
stakeholder governments can get together and essentially sign
"treaties"; these agreements create organizations, like a regional
economic development association, that work outside of traditional government channels. Less often, state governments get
involved—remember, local governments are created by states—to
develop new institutions, like authorities or councils, that have the
force of law.

Probably the most famous example of this kind of treaty is the
Port Authority of New York and New Jersey (PA), an unusual
interstate compact that oversees most of the transportation infrastructure around New York City. The 1921 agreement between
the two named states established a special "port authority district"
roughly centered on the Statue of Liberty, and created an organization that runs all the bridges, tunnels, and airports around the
metropolitan area. It also runs New York City's huge bus station,
which, probably for most people, the actual term "Port Authority"
refers to.

The PA (the authority, not the bus station) is enormous, influential, and *not* what regional cooperation supporters usually have
in mind when they advocate for local governments to interact. For
one, the PA's historical importance in the development of New
York City's infrastructure came at the cost of democratic control—
critics have complained about the authority's insular board for
decades. Primarily, the PA has been viewed as a political tool of
the two state governors: most notably, in the 2013 "Bridgegate"
scandal, staffers of New Jersey governor Chris Christie got the PA
to interfere with bridge traffic to punish a nearby mayor who had
been insufficiently supportive of Christie's political program.

Regional cooperation advocates more often look to Portland,
Oregon's "Metro Council," the country's first—and only—directly
elected regional government. The Metro Council consists of a

region-wide president, financial auditor, and six district council members, all gaining office through nonpartisan elections every four years. Unusually for a regional government, the council has its own dedicated funding source coming from fees and property taxes. It serves three counties and twenty-four cities, including Portland.

The Metro Council is seen largely as a successful model for regional governance. Its main achievement, at least according to the *Place Matters* authors, has been limiting sprawl. They argue that the council has been instrumental in ensuring limits on development, encouraging investments in public transit, and promoting other efforts to help Portland's downtown area stay a vibrant contributor to the local economy. Of course, the council has succeeded in part by aiming low, staying away from many of the area's most controversial issues like affordable housing and public schools. It also helps that Portland's metropolitan area was and remains relatively homogenous demographically, with significantly less racial tension than elsewhere.

Metro's example, then, suggests certain limits to how successful regional cooperation efforts might be in other parts of the country. Many regional bodies have no independent political base. Regional officials are most often appointed by mayors, governors, and county supervisors, and so may be perceived as owing allegiance to their benefactors instead of the people. Because they often lack a popular mandate, regional organizations end up focusing on very narrow, often technical issues or infrastructure. The city of St. Louis has a regional authority, for example, but its sole purpose is to manage the area's zoo.

And unfortunately, one of the main reasons regionalism is so important—that it could help protect an area's poor from the "race to the bottom"—remains a hard sell in American politics. Getting cities and counties to work together to make their entire region more hospitable to lower-income folks can drive worries that they are actively attracting more "unemployables." Of course, low-income people are not as mobile as some think; critics often seem to imply the nation's poor spend their days looking through travel brochures, concluding "Let's all move to Topeka and get welfare!" But there are probably at least *some* effects on migration if a city or county offers more support than other areas.

Regional efforts therefore have to overcome powerful incentives in American politics that divide local governments. Decades of white flight have fueled a city-versus-county mentality whereby lower-income minorities are seen as a city's problem and not the concern of its majority-white suburbs. But it is not just suburban counties that present barriers to cooperation. City leaders, who in many cases owe their political power to coalitions that speak for minorities, may come to enjoy the political promise that city services offer. Not only can they win votes by delivering services to poor communities, but the city agencies that deliver these services offer powerful patronage opportunities—a mayor can reward supporters with jobs in the city bureaucracy. And so the inertia of existing political interests in both city and county may be hard to overcome. As one former council member, Curtis Johnson, said about Portland's Metro: "If we didn't have it [already], we couldn't get a bill to create it passed."

The good news, at least for regionalism, is that suburban diversity has increased. Many suburban counties and towns are finding themselves having more and more in common with cities as population growth, denser development, and accompanying economic pressures come to the 'burbs. This phenomenon of urban-style development in a suburban county is sometimes referred to by the term "edge city." Tysons Corner is often held up as the ultimate example of such an edge city: it is an unincorporated area in Virginia's Fairfax County, near Washington, DC, but faces the same challenges as any cultural and economic center due to its increasing density and rapid growth. If more counties begin to look like cities, the obstacles to cooperation between the two may considerably lessen.

In addition, some powerful players have begun to recognize the importance of regional collaboration. In 2016, business leaders in Virginia, backed by Governor Terry McAuliffe, got the state legislature to fund a regionally based economic development program. "GO Virginia" distributes grants through a network of regional councils and aims to spur collaborations among local businesses, educational institutions, and governments in select regions of the state. The initiative is right out of the "power elite" theorist's playbook, with business and governmental leaders calling the shots. But at least those elites are steering resources away from the economic pressures that pit local governments against each other and toward regional solutions.

One final note: in his book, Peterson noted how some economists argued against local governments' efforts to recruit *specific* companies and industries. Sure, it would be nice to land a big fish like an auto plant, a brewing facility, or even Amazon's HQ2. But industry trends wax and wane—today's hot new thing becomes tomorrow's "disrupted" industry. These economists thought local governments would instead be smart to work on developing a *network* of public and private services for businesses and their workers. These include technical support like IT companies, professional services like attorneys and accountants, and public and private investment, but also good schools and transit options—essentially, an *infrastructure* to attract all sorts of companies and industries. Regions may be even better suited to develop and market such an infrastructure, as they can combine the resources and features of multiple localities.

Of course, just like any of the solutions described in this book, regionalism is no magic bullet. It will not solve every problem facing local governments, and it requires thoughtful design and citizen oversight to make sure there is accountability. But regional cooperation is one of the best ways to overcome a fundamental problem facing local governments. On the great "desert island" television drama *Lost*, characters would often remind one another that they would either "live together or die alone." Local governments are not exactly on a desert island, but their situation—being placed in a potentially fierce competition for scarce resources—is very similar. And so they also need to work together or face a similarly terrible fate.

SUMMARY

- Scholars debated the question of <u>who governs</u> in a city, with some favoring elites over "plural" interests, and others weighing the role of structure against agency.
- Paul Peterson settled on the idea of a locality having <u>interests</u>: political power, social prestige, and especially <u>economic position.</u>
- The structure of economic pressures leads localities to attract <u>export industries</u>—companies that make or sell things that bring in outside money.
- BUT this means localities <u>compete</u> for these export businesses and for "good" (high-skilled) workers. This leads to a <u>race to the bottom</u> characterized by giveaways and inequality.
- Localities can lessen competition and increase collaboration through <u>regional cooperation;</u> local governments can work together to lure in business and solve other problems as well.

ACTION STEPS

- *Support efforts to build regional cooperation.*
- *Avoid major giveaways to lure in specific businesses/industries.*
- *Support development of broad infrastructure.*

WANT TO KNOW MORE?

The beginning of John Mollenkopf's 1994 book about New York City politics, *A Phoenix in the Ashes*, does a good job of telling the story of the community power debate. (Full disclosure: I studied with Mollenkopf while I was getting my PhD.) Also, Mollenkopf's textbook *The Urban Politics Reader* (written with Elizabeth A.

Strom), is over a decade old but still offers a solid introduction to urban/local politics.

Not everyone tells the story of the development of urban politics scholarship in the same way I do. "Public choice" theories, for example, are an enormous influence in studies of local governance just as in other areas of political science; political economists like Charles Tiebout, Robert Warren, and Elinor and Vincent Ostrom characterized local governments as markets where rational actors make individual choices. For just one alternative account of the scholarship on local government, which includes public choice and other traditions, see chapter 2 of Kathryn Foster's *The Political Economy of Special-Purpose Government*.

As I noted above, the Port Authority of New York and New Jersey is in many ways a case study of how *not* to do regional cooperation. But that is partly because New York City is such a huge, dynamic, and complicated city, and it seems like the rules do not always apply there. (I lived there for a decade, and I can tell you from experience that this is certainly how New Yorkers sometimes feel about their home.) For a superb critical history of the Port Authority, read Jameson W. Doig's *Empire on the Hudson*.

Oregon's Metro Council maintains historical records and archives, some of which are posted online on their website https://www.oregonmetro.gov/metro-archives-and-special-collections. The Curtis Johnson quote above comes from Nate Berg's 2012 *CityLab* article, "The Only Elected Regional Government in the U.S." You can also check out another oft-cited example of regional governance, the Minneapolis–Saint Paul Metropolitan Council, at https://metrocouncil.org/; this council is similar to Portland's but is not directly elected. And you can read about the Saint Louis Zoo Authority here: https://www.stlzoo.org/about/organization/. (My favorite line: "Essentially, the Zoo is a government agency.")

The term "edge city" was likely coined by reporter Joel Garreau in his influential 1991 book *Edge City: Life on the New*

Frontier. Tysons Corner, along with Florida's Kendall–Dadeland area and Illinois's Chicago–adjacent Schaumburg, are all edge cities profiled in 2015's *Sequel to Suburbia*, an important study by London-based scholar Nick Phelps.

BIBLIOGRAPHY/FURTHER READING

Banfield, Edward C. 1961. *Political Influence*. New York: The Free Press.

Berg, Nate. 2012. "The Only Elected Regional Government in the U.S." *CityLab*. March 1. https://www.citylab.com/equity/2012/03/only-elected-regional-government-us/1371/.

"Bussed out: How America Moves Thousands of Homeless People around the Country." 2017. *The Guardian*. December 20. http://www.theguardian.com/us-news/ng-interactive/2017/dec/20/bussed-out-america-moves-homeless-people-country-study.

Dahl, Robert A. 1961. *Who Governs?* New Haven, CT: Yale University Press.

Doig, Jameson W. 2001. *Empire on the Hudson: Entrepreneurial Vision and Political Power at the Port of New York Authority*. New York: Columbia University Press.

Dreier, Peter, John Mollenkopf, and Todd Swanstrom. 2014. *Place Matters: Metropolitics for the Twenty First Century*. Third Edition Revised. Lawrence, KS: University Press of Kansas.

Foster, Kathryn A. 1997. *The Political Economy of Special-Purpose Government*. Washington, DC: Georgetown University Press.

Garreau, Joel. 1991. *Edge City: Life on the New Frontier*. New York: Anchor Books.

Hunter, Floyd. 1953. *Community Power Structure: A Study of Decision Makers*. Chapel Hill: University of North Carolina Press.

Mills, C. Wright. 1956. *The Power Elite*. New York: Oxford University Press.

Mollenkopf, John H. 1994. *A Phoenix in the Ashes: The Rise and Fall of the Koch Coalition in New York City Politics*. Princeton, NJ: Princeton University Press.

Peterson, Paul E. 1981. *City Limits*. Chicago: University of Chicago Press.

Phelps, Nicholas A. 2015. *Sequel to Suburbia: Glimpses of America's Post-Suburban Future*. Cambridge, MA: MIT Press.

Strom, Elizabeth A., and John H. Mollenkopf. 2007. *The Urban Politics Reader*. New York: Routledge.

DO NOT CUT SPENDING (TOO MUCH)

As noted earlier in this book, the story of local government in recent decades is all about *increased capacity*: local governments are providing expanded and new services in all sorts of policy areas. We ask our counties and cities to provide safe roads, law enforcement, fire departments, schools, and much, much more.

One big problem: no one wants to pay for it.

Americans have always had a problem with taxes. We all know that the American Revolution was triggered in part by "taxation without representation." (Never mind that the British were taxing colonists in part to pay for the expensive wars and military actions that had kept the colonies safe from France and angry-for-some-reason Native Americans.) But even before that, tax collecting in Europe had traditionally been a profession for brutes, rife with abuse of authority. American ideals of liberty and free enterprise, then as now, were not exactly aligned with forking over hard-earned money to government stooges.

And so politicians often appeal to this anti-tax tradition when they run for office. This is as true in local politics as it is at the national level. Candidates for mayor, county supervisor, or even local agricultural commissioner promise to slash spending, cut "waste," and make sure your tax dollars are protected or even returned to you. Of course, there is nothing wrong with making government more efficient! Local governments may be doing more, but it is true that the actual skill level and sophistication of government officials and staff are not always up to the job. As with any bureaucratic organization, local governments could probably tighten procedures and use their resources more wisely.

Still, candidates and officials can take this line of thinking too far. Smart local leaders know that cities and counties actually need to provide effective services and require the staff and budget to be able to support those services. Parks, schools, libraries, and even programs for lower-income families are part of what makes a neighborhood a good place to live; if you cut spending *too* much in a municipality, then no one is going to want to live there.

This chapter will make a case that is not often popular in American politics—that *more* spending and *higher* taxes some-times can be better for everyone.

BUREAUCRATIC MYTHS

"Government waste" is, for some, a redundant phrase. This can be especially true in local government, thanks to the massive expansion of budgets and functions over the past few decades. There are plenty of examples of poorly managed programs and offices, or corrupt local officials spending money on boondoggles and cronies. Local government staff and capacity have grown, but the level of professional knowledge and skill has not always kept up.

Take just one important government function: contracting and procurement. Just like any organization, local governments "procure" or buy supplies and services from a variety of vendors. These supplies can range from paper clips to massive vehicles like garbage trucks and bulldozers, and services can cover cleaning the city council's bathrooms as well as operating a multimillion-dollar IT/computer infrastructure. But local procurement offices are often understaffed and overwhelmed, even when they have enough funding. For example, the federal Department of Homeland Security established a taskforce in 2004 to try to figure out why local governments were not ramping up their security infrastructure in response to the 9/11 attacks, despite a pile of new federal money being available. The taskforce's final report basically concluded that many local governments simply could not handle the money—they did not have the necessary infrastructure or staff to deal with federal grant regulations and reimbursement processes.

Then there is the problem of seemingly rampant criminality. We may no longer have corrupt leaders like the infamous Boss Tweed, who used his control of the Tammany political machine in nineteenth-century New York to bilk the city of millions in construction dollars. But the same methods remain, especially if a local government does not have the proper controls in place to prevent them. In early 2019, for instance, *The New York Times* reported on how corruption scandals were developing in four of the country's greatest cities, with stories ranging from a Philadelphia councilman who seemed to be on the payroll of a local union boss to a deputy chief of staff in Atlanta who allegedly received bribes from a vendor.

But you can find corruption outside of the big cities as well. In 2012, the comptroller of Dixon, Illinois, was convicted of embezzling over $50 million from a city of just 15,000 residents; some called this episode the heftiest municipal theft in history. Corruption also doesn't have to involve sizeable amounts of money. In 2017, the clerk of the tiny town of Hallwood, Virginia, responded to an audit request from town officials by resigning. However, she also loaded all of the town records into her car, which then suffered a mysterious fire that burned all the records! Unsurprisingly, the clerk was arrested two years later on sixty-five charges of embezzlement. But the amount she allegedly stole was less than $25,000.

These incidents are actually quite rare when you consider the sheer number of local governments. But they feed headlines and provoke citizen outrage of far greater proportions than their actual occurrence warrants. In general, Americans have a low opinion of government bureaucrats, considering them both corrupt and lazy. Policy scholars sometimes call these "bureaucratic myths." Americans often believe that government is always wasteful, driven largely by inefficient, lazy employees. The classic image of the government bureaucrat is the glassy-eyed functionary at the DMV who tells you that you have been in the wrong line for the past four hours, and "Could you please provide six forms of ID?"

In reality, there is little evidence to support this negative view of public employees. Multiple studies have shown that "government bureaucracy" is composed of competent, dedicated employees in the same proportion as any other industry. Public-sector employees may be more driven by "intrinsic" benefits like mission and service as opposed to compensation and promotion, but they are just as hardworking as anyone else. As for inefficiency, there is actually little evidence to show that private-sector companies are any more efficient than government. How often have you praised the prompt and friendly service provided to you by your local cable company? Or the fantastic and useful array of services offered by our popular and beloved airlines?

When private companies *are* efficient, often they get there by being much more ruthless than we would want. Saying that "government should be more like business" often means that government should also not pay a living wage or cost-of-living increases, that it should cut benefits to employees or engage in "wage theft" by limiting breaks and not paying overtime, or that it should cut corners on products and services to save costs, even if it risks customer injury and death. If you think government does a bad job, you should check out how private, for-profit prisons operate: not only are they *not* more efficient than public-sector prisons, but they often show little regard for inmates as actual human beings, resulting in worse outcomes. A 2016 report from the federal Department of Justice concluded that contract prisons had more safety and security incidents than government-run prisons, and were much more likely to feature improper security and housing procedures.

Most evidence suggests that privatization will not remove inefficiency from government. In general, large bureaucratic organizations, public *or* private, are going to feature *some* amount of waste and inefficiency; this is unavoidable given the scope and scale of what they are trying to accomplish. There is always the possibility that there is a mid-level supervisor who seems to care more about employee breaks than the quality of their work, or that team member who never comes to meetings but takes credit for the final project, whether you work in business *or* government. But it is typically only when people are asked to pay higher taxes that they think this kind of inefficiency is an unforgivable offense.

And just like everything else in urban politics, there is a racial element underlying myths about bureaucracy. As we will see in the next chapter, much of the civil rights movement involved local battles for equal access to city services. African Americans won this fight in part by gaining representation and equal opportunity; basically, they got elected and got hired in cities throughout the country. Segregationists found it much harder to maintain the informal hiring discrimination in the public sector that kept minorities out of other professions; so in many cities with sizeable minority populations, African Americans flocked to public-sector jobs.

The result? Many urban areas have bureaucracies filled with black, middle-class employees, who are however especially prone to being characterized by myths about corruption and waste. Due to explicit and implicit racial bias, white citizens are much more likely to downplay how much of their taxes goes toward paying for necessary services like parks, law enforcement, and health clinics. Instead, they often characterize their taxes as forced transfers to "lazy, corrupt bureaucrats," who just happen to be the same "lazy, shiftless" people white Americans have always scapegoated, especially in the South.

Put together all of these components—a history of racial animus, a general distrust of bureaucracy, a few high-profile corruption scandals, and Americans' general dislike of paying taxes—and you have a nice recipe for a lot of grumbling about local government bureaucracy. You also get a blueprint for local politicians: win support and elections by promising to cut taxes and spending. No more bureaucrats wasting your money!

But that is exactly when you need to resist that siren call. Because here is the truth: a local government cannot cut its way to prosperity.

Think of it this way: why do you live where you live? Of course, not everyone is as mobile as economists often assume. But people who *can* choose where to live generally do not pick a city or county based on the tax rate. Instead, they want to live where there are job and educational opportunities, as well as amenities and services—parks and libraries, arts and culture, and successful public schools. People—even rich people—want to live in a place *that is a good place to live*. Ideally, of course, everyone would also want to live in a place that is equitable, that treats all citizens well and provides for the needs of the most vulnerable. But even the worst, most stereotypically heartless billionaire plutocrat does not want to have to step over homeless people on the way to work. Even these folks want a safe, exciting, and interesting neighborhood, with a thriving economy and rich cultural scene.

If you do elect a silver-tongued politician who follows through on their promise to cut spending, you will probably end up regretting it. Sure, a lot of local government services go toward helping the poor. They're poor! They need stuff like health clinics, welfare and social service offices, job training, and other forms of support. Maybe you are a heartless person who does not care if there are no shelters for the homeless. But what if the city suddenly does not have the staff to fix potholes or clear snow from side streets? What if there is more trash on county lanes thanks to less frequent garbage truck runs? What if the town library is no longer open on weekends or the local public schools cannot seem to afford to offer a girls' lacrosse team this year?

The bottom line: you get what you pay for.

CONSIDER THE LIBRARY

Let's look at one classic example of a local government service: the good old public library. Kicked off by early investment from philanthropists like Andrew Carnegie in the mid-nineteenth century, taxpayer-funded libraries became a staple of most cities and counties by the early 1900s. Today, almost all counties and municipalities feature at least some form of a public library system. Although the role of public libraries has changed especially in the past few decades, many people still think of them as merely local book lenders. This stereotype is prevalent enough that a misguided economist wrote in *Forbes* in 2018 that Amazon and online booksellers should be able to make public libraries obsolete. The online response was swift and fierce—in general, the first rule of libraries is "Thou shalt not tick off the librarians"—as staffers and users alike pointed out how outdated this idea was.

For an example, take Warren County Public Library, a small four-branch library system located near Bowling Green, Kentucky. (You may not believe me, but I chose this library literally at random through a simple web search.) In just one week in June 2019, this system offered the following:

- Early childhood programs, including story times for children of at least three different levels (from babies to preschool), plus a bilingual English–Spanish program and an American Sign Language class for babies;
- Art and "young inventor" programs for teens and tweens, plus embroidery and pottery for adults;
- An introductory session about the library's 3D printer, open to all ages;
- Yoga, with separate sessions for children and adults;
- Off-site gatherings for the library's summer reading program, including a book talk by an astronaut and a kickoff celebration at the local science museum.

All of these programs were offered in addition to the system's year-round book and video lending, plus free audio, e-books, and streaming available through the library website. This may sound like a cherry-picked busy week at some kind of overachieving, fancy library. But with all due respect to the Warren County libraries, this array of services and programs is actually not all that special. Warren is not a poor county, but it is not a rich one either; in terms of local income, it's pretty average. A number of library systems in localities—both wealthy and not-so-wealthy—all across the country offer similar services and programs, all funded by local taxes, to local citizens.

Maybe you are not interested in these programs or, like the *Forbes* economist above, think it is better for people who want such services to pay for them directly. Why should your taxes fund someone else's book hobby, 3D printer session, or yoga class? That's fine—you can be a Scrooge if you want to—but many people would seem to disagree with you. According to an annual survey by the nonprofit Institute of Museum and Library Services, over 170 million Americans—almost half of us—made over *one billion visits* to public libraries in 2016.

Not all of those visits are about enrichment classes, though. Yoga and story time can be fun and can enhance anyone's life. But libraries are also essential providers of necessary resources for local residents, particularly those with low incomes. Story time is more than just a way to entertain your toddler for an hour; these kinds of programs help develop literacy. For families without disposable income for books and the like, the classes and other resources offered by libraries help broaden educational opportunities for everyone.

And libraries offer benefits in areas beyond education. Millions of Americans still lack access to broadband Internet, especially in rural areas, and many low-income families cannot afford home computers. Libraries have become a central place for these folks to conduct the normal business of digital life: kids are doing home-work while adults are paying bills, gathering information, and checking emails. By providing access to computers and training on how to use them, libraries have become important cogs in the machine of local workforce development, helping to cultivate digital literacy and valuable job skills. Some libraries even offer more specific employment education, including interview skills training and entrepreneurship classes.

Libraries provide so many of these kinds of benefits, in fact, that Texas's state libraries commissioned a report in 2017 from the University of Texas–Austin to try to quantify them. The report concluded that for every dollar invested in libraries, communities got back $4.64 in access to resources, technology, and staff support.

Now, I have suggested in other chapters that we should be skeptical of economic "impact," and it seems absurdly precise to say that $4.64 is the correct number. Still, the evidence is fairly clear that libraries provide significant benefits to the local communities that invest tax dollars in them.

Finally, there is a less quantifiable benefit from having a central place in a community where residents can come together. The resulting social networking can be almost accidental, like when you happen to see your neighbors at a yoga class or when children meet new friends at a story time session. But it can also be more specifically targeted, like when libraries offer free meeting spaces for local civic organizations, advocacy groups, and government commissions and committees. Libraries are often centrally located within a county or city and accessible via public transport, and they are often places with which many citizens are already familiar. Having a community space where different people come together can be important for building a democratic society. As sociologist Eric Klinenberg argued in his 2018 book *Palaces for the People*, such shared community spaces can help bridge the polarizing political and social divides that seem to have been accentuated and reinforced by so much of modern life.

And yet we tend to take all of these possible benefits for granted. Library funding nationwide was slashed considerably after the 2008 financial crisis, with many budgets never fully recovering. Politicians overlook these benefits when they bash bureaucracies, even if they are not specifically targeting libraries. And that is the thing: however much return on investment we get from libraries, these benefits are not entirely free. You still need to fund the technology and materials that are used to provide all of these resources, the buildings that house them, and the staff who make programs happen.

Libraries are just one example of the many, many services that local government provides. Not all of them offer as big a bang for your buck as libraries do, but almost all of them were developed in response to an important need from the community. We should *not* resent paying for those needs to be addressed, especially if we get a greater return in benefits.

REAL SOLUTIONS TO "WASTE"

So if we need to accept a certain amount of taxation to support necessary services from local government, does that mean we should also accept corruption and waste? Well, not exactly.

As I noted above, you *do* have to accept that large bureaucratic organizations will have *some* inefficiencies. If you run into a delay in getting a construction permit or find yourself frustrated with the incompetence of a town clerk, you can complain all you want. Just do not go overboard: the existence of an occasional problem in government does not mean the whole enterprise is doomed. There are plenty of helpful people dedicated to their government service jobs whom you will probably also encounter in your life; we just naturally downplay these normal, efficient experiences in favor of the outrageous outliers.

But corruption, waste, and inefficiency are still there and we should still do *something* about them, even if we should not dramatically cut spending and services. Luckily, there are things we can do that make more sense than spending cuts; "starving the beast" is not as effective as increasing transparency, accountability, and efficiency through other means. Other options that local governments can implement to improve performance include the following:

- **E-government**: technology has contributed dramatically to the increased capacity of local governments, and there are some promising innovations that can help govern- ments do their job even more effectively and efficiently.

These tech solutions go well beyond paying tickets and utility bills online, although these are welcome changes from dragging yourself down to the courthouse or utility office. Some states and localities are implementing community "dashboards" that publicly track budget data and performance goals: Michigan, for example, requires cities and counties to publish this kind of information before they are eligible to receive funds from state grants.

- **Performance budgeting**: an idea that goes back to the 1950s, performance-based budgeting is a tool that gets departments and bureaucrats to worry less about maintaining funding levels from last year and more about achieving their goals for this year. This approach helps governments allocate funding in flexible ways, rewarding innovation and achievement. More and more, local governments are being pushed to implement similar efforts by either state legislation or their own desire to improve budgeting and performance.

- **(Limited) privatization**: as I hinted above when talking about prisons, I am generally skeptical of the merits of privatizing central government services—the results of such efforts, looking at schools and prisons, are mixed at best. But outsourcing and privatizing more specialized tasks make plenty of sense: there is a longstanding tradition of government contracting that is not always bad. Officials need to tread lightly here, but not every local government needs a payroll department, for example, or a full-time cleaning staff. Local and state governments can help by keeping tight controls on contracting rules, like limiting the no-bid contracts that are often used to funnel money to well-connected political pals.

- **Auditing**: local governments, especially those in larger cities and counties, can also help keep an eye on contracting and budgeting through a robust auditing office. It helps, too, if the auditor is viewed as a helpful collaborator of department heads and not a prosecutor looking to generate headlines by finding heads to roll.

- **Local journalism**: this is an old tool, not new, and one that exists outside of government. But a vibrant local press is absolutely essential for keeping tabs on government over-reach and corruption, as well as for calling out the most egregious inefficiencies. If you have a local newspaper and you can afford to subscribe, do it, even if only digitally. Even responding positively on social media to solid investigative reporting from print, radio, or television reports, might encourage journalists to produce more of it.

All of these solutions would be made easier by public officials who are willing and able to do the hard work of managing a bureaucracy. Whether you have a strong-mayor system with a single head of the executive branch, or a weak-mayor system where the legislative branch (the council or board) is responsible for administration as well, you need capable leaders who take their oversight duties seriously. And this kind of oversight, not cutting and slashing government, should be the focus of political officials and candidates. Better auditing and more transparency may not be as politically popular to talk about as cutting taxes. But a focus on effective bureaucracy is more honest about effects and benefits, and is better for local communities. With local government, as with anything else, if you want nice things—and most of us do— you have to be willing to pay for them.

SUMMARY

- Although Americans have a generally negative opinion of bureaucracy, most <u>local government bureaucrats</u> are <u>dedicated and effective</u>.
- Politicians who make popular arguments for <u>cutting government spending</u> can be <u>short-sighted</u>; local governments <u>need funds</u> to support <u>necessary services</u> like parks, roads, and libraries.
- <u>Libraries</u>, for example, provide a host of <u>benefits</u> to local communities, from <u>literacy</u> and <u>digital access</u> to <u>workforce development</u>.
- Local governments can improve efficiency and reduce corruption and waste through a variety of initiatives that promote <u>accountability</u> and <u>transparency</u>.

ACTION STEPS

- *Avoid candidates and officials who argue for slashing spending and cutting services, or who demonize bureaucrats as lazy and wasteful.*
- *Support reasonable and relatively efficient public spending on necessary services like parks, roads, libraries, and social services.*
- *Support initiatives to provide more efficient services such as e-government, performance budgets, and careful auditing.*

WANT TO KNOW MORE?

Government "waste" is often about contracting and procurement. The National Association of State Procurement Officials (NASPO), a professional organization of mostly state-level contracting officers, produces a guide for local bureaucrats that offers a window into how this whole procurement thing works.

A 2006 *Journal of Public Administration Research and Theory* article features a well-cited comparative study of the values of public-sector and private-sector workers. For more recent research, you could check out a similar 2014 study in *VOLUNTAS: The International Journal of Voluntary and Nonprofit Organizations*, among many, many others.

Private prisons have come under a lot of scrutiny in recent years. Noah Smith, an opinion writer for Bloomberg News, published in April 2019 a nice summary of some of the problems with contracting for prison services.

Public libraries, on the other hand, have much more support. The American Library Association website (http://www.ala.org/) is full of arguments and data about the benefits of libraries; you also can find tons of academic research in journals like *The Library Quarterly* and *Library & Information Science Research*. For a more narrative approach, Susan Orlean's *The Library Book* tells the story of libraries while focusing on a 1986 fire at the Los Angeles Public Library.

You can also find a lot of research on innovations in government accountability and efficiency. E-government, for example, is the subject of many articles published in the mid-2000s, as local governments across the globe embraced new technology. The area of e-government has grown enough that there is now a textbook, *E-Government and Information Technology Management: Concepts and Best Practices*, which offers a dry but comprehensive introduction to the scope of research and practice. Performance budgeting has a similar literature from the same time period; a more recent article that shows the scope of and challenges facing these budgeting practices appeared in *Public Performance & Management Review* in 2017.

I mentioned "news deserts" and the ongoing death of local news in an earlier chapter. New initiatives like States Newsroom (https://statesnewsroom.com/), a national network of nonprofit news organizations supported by philanthropy, may suggest a way forward.

BIBLIOGRAPHY/FURTHER READING

Beale, Lewis. 2017. "How Ronald Reagan's Hometown Was Robbed Blind." *The Daily Beast*, August 14. https://www.thedailybeast.com/how-ronald-reagans-hometown-was-robbed-blind.

Cicoira, Linda. 2019. "Former Hallwood Clerk Charged with Embezzlement." *Eastern Shore Post*. February 7. http://www.easternshorepost.com/2019/02/07/full-story-former-hallwood-clerk-charged-with-embezzlement/.

Fausset, Richard, Monica Davey, and Tim Arango. 2019. "'It's the Human Way': Corruption Scandals Play Out in Big Cities Across U.S." *The New York Times*, February 5. https://www.nytimes.com/2019/02/05/us/fbi-corruption-investigations.html.

Ha, Thu-Huong. 2018. "Forbes Deleted a Deeply Misinformed Op-Ed Arguing Amazon Should Replace Libraries." *Quartz*. July 23. https://qz.com/1334123/forbes-deleted-an-op-ed-arguing-that-amazon-should-replace-libraries/.

Hijal-Moghrabi, Imane. 2017. "The Current Practice of Performance-Based Budgeting in the Largest U.S. Cities: An Innovation Theory Perspective." *Public Performance & Management Review* 40 (4): 652–75. https://doi.org/10.1080/15309576.2017.1313168.

Holzer, Marc, Aroon Manoharan, and James Melitski. 2019. *E-Government and Information Technology Management: Concepts and Best Practices.* Irvine, CA: Melvin & Leigh.

Homeland Security Advisory Council. 2004. "A Report from the Task Force on State and Local Homeland Security Funding." Washington, DC: U.S. Department of Homeland Security.

Jarrett, James. 2017. "Texas Public Libraries: Economic Benefits and Return on Investment." Austin: Texas State Libraries and Archive Commission.

Klinenberg, Eric. 2018. *Palaces for the People: How Social Infrastructure Can Help Fight Inequality, Polarization, and the Decline of Civic Life*. New York: Crown/Archetype.

Miller-Stevens, Katrina, Jennifer A. Taylor, and John C. Morris. 2015. "Are We Really on the Same Page? An Empirical Examination of Value Congruence between Public Sector and Nonprofit Sector Managers." *VOLUNTAS: The International Journal of Voluntary and Nonprofit Organizations* 26 (6): 2424–2446. https://doi.org/10.1007/s11266-014-9514-6.

National Association of State Procurement Officials. 2019. "NASPO State and Local Procurement: A Practical Guide." Lexington, KY: National Association of State Procurement Officials.

Orlean, Susan. 2019. *The Library Book*. London: Atlantic Books.

"Review of the Federal Bureau of Prisons' Monitoring of Contract Prisons." 2016. Washington, DC: U.S. Department of Justice, Office of the Inspector General.

Smith, Noah. 2019. "Private Prisons Are a Failed Experiment." *Bloomberg*, April 1. https://www.bloomberg.com/opinion/articles/2019-04-01/u-s-private-prisons-are-a-failed-government-experiment.

Stackman, Richard W., Patrick E. Connor, and Boris W. Becker. 2006. "Sectoral Ethos: An Investigation of the Personal Values Systems of Female and Male Managers in the Public and Private Sectors." *Journal of Public Administration Research and Theory* 16 (4): 577–97. https://doi.org/10.1093/jopart/mui059.

SUPPORT RACIAL DIVERSITY AND EQUITY

With apologies to feminism, the post-war fight for black civil rights is probably the most successful political movement in American history. Unlike the bloody Civil War, which basically reset the Southern political structure from an official to an unofficial apartheid regime, the disruptive actions of black activists and their allies in the decades after World War II dramatically reshaped racial relations in American society. Although claims of a "post-racial society" are overstated, the fact is that discrimination is much rarer than in the past, and opportunity for people of color has expanded considerably.

One point that is often overlooked, though, is that the civil rights movement was largely *a fight against local governments*. Sure, the chief victories of the movement were federal laws and agencies protecting voting rights and banning discrimination, but many of the targets of those laws were local registrars and public officials in cities and counties throughout the country. Before and during the civil rights movement, local governments were often on the frontline of racial disparities and attempts to overcome them; they remain significant battlegrounds for diversity and equality today.

We often have people tell us that diversity matters, but we do not often hear *why* it matters. It matters because our representatives need to make sure that all members of a community have a voice, and that laws and regulations are implemented in a fair and equitable manner. Equal treatment under the law is a bedrock ideal of modern democracy. If, as I have argued throughout this book, local governments are doing more and what they do is important, then ensuring racial diversity and equity at the local level is just as important as any nationwide crusade. In addition, the long history of American racism is intertwined with local governments.

You *cannot* write a book about local politics and leave race out of it.

I wish this were not true; I wish that we really, truly lived in a post-racial, color-blind society. But the truth is that our lingering racial history undermines almost every other "right answer" in this book, from public transportation to support for public services. Local government demands diversity, both in elected office and the bureaucracy, to help overcome still-strong segregation and inequality, and to make sure that the benefits and opportunities of local politics are open to all.

A HISTORY OF LOCAL RACISM

It is well outside the scope of this book to try to do any kind of justice to the long history of racial discrimination in America. Suffice it to say that the country has been more than a little unkind to people of color, particularly African Americans. For centuries, slavery, often called America's "original sin," and the century of Jim Crow laws in the South (and continued discrimination elsewhere) completely undermined the ability of many blacks to live as full citizens.

This history of racial discrimination is embedded in the evolution of local governance in a way that is often overlooked. Two important historical episodes, one being more of a fiasco and the other more triumphant, help explain why race is so important to local politics even today. I briefly describe these episodes below.

Post-War Urban Renewal

In the chapter on public transportation above, I mentioned the "urban renewal" campaigns of the mid-twentieth century. But the scope of these efforts, which involved collaboration between the federal government and local governments, went well beyond the promotion of suburban growth through highway and road development. In the years following World War II, the country's leaders became more and more concerned with the "urban crisis." Cities were starting to find themselves left out of the burgeoning growth of the U.S. As America started moving from its manufacturing base to more of a service economy, work became less concentrated in urban factories and more dispersed among smaller facilities often located in newly growing suburbs. As I noted earlier, the federal transportation dollars that went toward building roads out to the suburbs instead of developing public transportation in the urban core did not help.

What also did not help was racial tension. Spurred in part by efforts at desegregation and by the dramatic migration of blacks from the rural South to urban centers all across the country, affluent whites were abandoning city centers. This "white flight" led to a declining tax base in cities, as well as growing minority populations often concentrated in urban slums and ghettos. The country's leaders eventually reached consensus on a diagnosis of the problem. In their view, poor neighborhoods were draining urban coffers because of the lack of economic development. What America's urban core needed was a revitalizing infusion of energy and funds. And so "urban renewal" was born.

Renewal, however, took on a particular flavor. This nationally led solution was not about workforce development and job creation, or innovation and investment. It was, as historian Francesca Russello Ammon called it in her 2016 book *Bulldozer*, a "culture of clearance." The post-war answer to urban problems was to clear away existing neighborhoods in favor of newly engineered communities.

In fairness to the reformers, there was a genuine optimism in the post-war period about reconstruction and technological know-how. The Americans had won the greatest war in history, had built their economy into a manufacturing powerhouse, and were already rebuilding Europe. Why not rebuild America's cities as well? On the other hand, the rebuilding movement swept away everything in its path, including growing communities and the start of a black middle class. Because some blacks lived in slums, any black neighborhood could be targeted as a "blighted" neighborhood and an appropriate site for new construction. Hardly any participant in the renewal effort could be bothered to actually ask the communities involved if they even wanted to be "renewed."

And so national government initiatives, like the Federal Housing Act of 1954 and the Department of Housing and Urban Development, created in 1965, were designed to work with cities to bulldoze local "slums" in favor of newly engineered housing "projects." Early on in the advent of urban renewal, even minority political leaders and social welfare advocates were hopeful that federal dollars would go toward developing new housing and other forms of support for economically disadvantaged communities. What national and local leaders were unable to see, however, is that by re-engineering the urban landscape, they were engaged in the wholesale destruction of existing neighborhoods, particularly those of lower-income minorities.

The resulting urban renewal efforts did end up transforming low-income neighborhoods, often dramatically. But because the federal programs placed few restrictions on what was to replace them, because there was little to no communication with the affected communities, and because local and federal governments alike offered minimal economic development opportunities for the recently built housing projects, urban renewal is considered by most observers today to be a total failure.

There are two major byproducts of this failed effort to help cities, both of which have had devastating effects on impoverished minorities—blacks in particular. First, it was an economic disaster for the nation's African American population. Urban renewal policies essentially undermined the economic development of an entire generation of blacks and other minorities, through geographic and social displacement and the destruction of decades of social capital. Combined with "redlining," or the widespread banking practice of refusing to provide mortgages to even economically qualified black families, these policies basically denied home ownership to a generation of African Americans, thus also depriving them of an invaluable opportunity to build wealth. The black middle class, just as it was starting to get an economic leg up thanks to civil rights activism, was effectively hollowed out in many cities by urban renewal.

The other negative effect of renewal was the exacerbation of racial tension across the country. The geographic displacement caused by renewal projects meant blacks had to find new places to live, causing increased tension and more white flight as more working-class and poor white neighborhoods were "invaded" by displaced blacks. Those minorities lucky enough to find homes in newly designed housing projects found themselves quickly abandoned by local governments and essentially living in homes of last resort. The resulting concentration of poverty and correlated problems like crime was reported in local media and government analyses in such a way as to reinforce damaging stereotypes of urban minorities. "We tried to help these people, and they still live like animals," became the not-always-unspoken subtext of urban renewal.

Civil Rights: A Local Movement

The story of race and local politics is not *all* bad. Urban renewal was a fiasco—yes—but it is not as if all people of color were helpless victims. Many fought back against urban renewal just as they had against oppression for centuries. And most of these fighters were engaged in a battle on a larger scale, one that is familiar to most Americans.

The civil rights movement is most often portrayed as a national phenomenon, with central figures like John Lewis, Fannie Lou Hamer, and of course, Martin Luther King, Jr. rightly celebrated as American heroes. The 1963 March on Washington is probably the single most famous moment from the civil rights era, and getting the Civil Rights and Voting Rights acts passed by Congress remains among the movement's crowning achievements. But though this national story is certainly an accurate one, the civil rights movement was just as much about efforts to reform local government.

Many movement actions involved local organizations that fought against oppressive municipal and county governments. The famous 1965 marches from Selma to Montgomery, for example, may have been organized by King's Southern Christian Leadership Conference (SCLC), but King and his group were invited to Montgomery in the first place by the local Dallas County Voters League, only after the local group's voter registration efforts had been frustrated by county officials and by the county chapter of the white supremacist Citizens' Council.

Other famous episodes of the movement similarly involved challenges to local governments:

- The famous bus boycott sparked in part by Rosa Parks's courageous activism in 1955 targeted the public transit system in the city of Montgomery, Alabama.
- In 1957, the governor of Arkansas famously used the National Guard to prevent black students from entering Little Rock Central High School until the federal government intervened. The governor may have been heavily involved in the school's eventual desegregation, but it was the local school district that had to deal with the fallout, and it was the district that eventually shut down, rather than fully integrating, its schools at the end of the year. This was a common practice elsewhere in the South and especially in Virginia, where "massive resistance" to racial equity encouraged Prince Edward County to close its public schools for *five full years*.
- As in Selma, county registrars throughout the South were the frontline soldiers against blacks' right to vote, employing tools like unfairly administered literacy tests to deny them registration. And as in Selma, when local and national groups started breaking through these obstacles, it was local Klan and Citizens' Council groups that fought back with violence.
- Martin Luther King, Jr. wrote his famous "Letter from a Birmingham Jail" from, well, a municipal jail in the city of Birmingham, Alabama. King had been arrested during the 1963 Birmingham Campaign, an effort to ensure that blacks were treated fairly and equally by downtown businesses. One of the more infamous villains of that campaign, Eugene "Bull" Connor, was the city's Commissioner of Public Safety—a municipal official.
- The civil rights movement was not just active in the South: one prominent action in 1962 called attention to the public school system in the City of Chester, Pennsylvania. One

black school in Chester had been built to hold 500 students, but instead had over 1,200, with only two functional bathrooms for the entire school. The local Committee for Freedom Now negotiated directly with city leadership and the school board to improve facility conditions, eventually winning court-ordered desegregation for the whole school district.

This local focus should not be surprising. Local governments were often the source of discriminatory practices and policies. The civil rights movement was about changing the culture of the entire country, but it also aimed to specifically change the discriminatory codes, written or otherwise, in cities, counties, and towns all across the nation.

Discrimination was not just about the denial of rights but, as in the Chester case above, the denial of city services as well. "Separate but equal" had been the nominal law of the land since 1896's *Plessy v. Ferguson* Supreme Court case, but the "equal" part had never been enforced. This was obviously true with school facilities, as public education became a key battleground in desegregation efforts. But it also applied to more mundane city services like garbage pickup and building permits, not to mention life-or-death needs like fire protection, law enforcement, and emergency care. All of these services were implemented by local governments in one way for whites and in another way for blacks. Just how long this imbalance continued is evidenced by the hip-hop group Public Enemy's song "911 Is a Joke," which resonated with black audiences who recognized how hard it was for emergency calls in black neighborhoods to get a response. What is even sadder is that the song was a hit in *1990*, over a hundred years since *Plessy* and three decades after nominal desegregation.

Alongside the civil rights movement's fight for national legislation and power was a battle for similar effects at the local level. Movement leaders recognized that white city and county leaders were not going to suddenly abandon discriminatory practices overnight, and that even the most well-meaning white allies in government still had minimal understanding of the black experience. And so the movement focused on winning political power—local offices, for sure, but also appointment power and anti-discrimination hiring reform. By getting blacks into government offices, the civil rights movement ensured that the people with power who either blindly or willingly discriminated against blacks would no longer be able to degrade or ignore black communities.

Knowingly or not, these leaders were advancing a theory of **descriptive representation**, the idea that the description of representatives should closely match that of their constituents. No matter how our government officials act, the theory goes, they nonetheless need to remain in some way similar to those they represent in order to govern fairly and effectively. And in fact, most data suggests that a more representative government is less discriminatory and more responsive to the needs of minority communities. As noted at the beginning of this book, part of the story of increased capacity is local governments finally serving the needs of all citizens, not just white ones; local governments have expanded in part because the civil rights movement finally forced them to do so.

There is plenty of evidence that minority representation has increased in local governments; for blacks in the South, especially, this was largely unavoidable once they truly won the right to vote. For example, the first black mayor of a major city was elected in 1967 (Carl Stokes in Cleveland); and when Maynard Jackson was elected in Atlanta in 1973, it felt like the dam was really breaking. By 2019, fifteen of the country's largest one hundred cities had a black mayor. And although data on local government officials is harder to gather, it is clear that minority representation has increased dramatically on city councils, county boards, and commissions, and in local bureaucracies across the South and the rest of the country.

In the decades that followed the heyday of civil rights, some minority candidates for local office even pursued a controversial strategy of **deracialization**. Advanced chiefly by political scientist Charles Hamilton in the 1970s, this strategy suggested that by reducing the prominence of racial appeals and minority concerns in general, black candidates can build successful white-majority coalitions that can still advance progressive policies to help minorities. This strategy was credited for several local electoral victories, particularly in the 1989 "Black Tuesday" election in which David Dinkins was chosen as mayor of New York City, among other victories in local elections across the country. Still, although deracialization may lead to increased black representation, many activists and observers worry that these victories come at the cost of the specific needs and concerns of minority communities.

The struggle for black civil rights continues today, even if many wish it were unnecessary. (If the problem of racial discrimination had been solved, there would have been no need for this chapter.) **#BlackLivesMatter** is more than just a hashtag: the term reflects a widespread movement involving local and national leaders who demand reform of local law enforcement. Again demonstrating the local roots of national movements, one of the triggering events for #BlackLivesMatter was the fatal shooting of a young African American man, Michael Brown, by a police officer from the city of Ferguson, Missouri. Protests and civil disruption in Ferguson became connected to more widespread activism that focused on not just the distressing number of high-profile murders of black men by police, but also discriminatory policies such as "stop-and-frisk." #BlackLivesMatter is a nationwide effort, but the targets of movement demands are most often the policies and practices of local government authorities. The saying "the more things change, the more they stay the same" may be a cliché, but it has been invoked more than once by black activists in recent years as they again demand changes from local governments.

SO WHAT DO WE DO?

OK, then, how do we end racism?

Well, that obviously cannot be accomplished by this little book. Still, there are ways to approach local politics that lessen the power of discrimination and make things better for everyone.

First—and given the sheer scale and history of oppression in this country, it is kind of sad that I have to state this—everyone has to continue to acknowledge the lingering effects of anti-black racism. There is a broad sense of fatigue in our culture (almost exclusively among whites, of course) when it comes to issues of race. Again invoking the idea of a "post-racial" America, these folks often ask: *If a black man could be elected president, surely our country has moved past our old problems? Can't everyone just get over it?* And yet race still infects our politics in ways that are both pervasive and subtle—although sometimes, as with #BlackLivesMatter and the continuing murders of black men by law enforcement, no subtlety is necessary.

And so, it helps to recognize the history of urban renewal, for example, when there is tension between a city and its nearby suburban counties. How much do local residents know about the displacement of black neighborhoods in the not-so-distant past? How can cities and counties work together to restore opportunities to economically disadvantaged minority families? Similarly, how much is distrust of local urban bureaucracies—which, as noted in the last chapter, is often infused with racial stereotypes—based in actual reality? How can cities do a better job of telling success stories of effective local governance, particularly if many of the people in local government are minorities?

One possible response to urban renewal, which continues today, includes **community empowerment** efforts adopted by a variety of locally based, grassroots organizations. Urban politics scholar Peter Dreier identified at least three different empowerment strategies employed by these groups over the past few decades. First, some groups offer **community-based service provision** for low-income minorities to overcome the opportunity gap, with services ranging from childcare to legal advice. Second, organizations can pursue **community-based development** efforts like the land trusts noted in the housing chapter above, or entrepreneurship or investment programs. Finally, **community organizing** covers a host of political mobilization efforts, from voter registration drives to advocacy training. Citizens and local governments alike can invest in these efforts and organizations through contracting, donations, and participation.

Also, everyone can support the recruitment and election of people of color to public office. Again, minority representation has increased dramatically since the days of segregation, but it still lags behind the demographics of constituents. In North Carolina, for example, a 2016 study by the think tank Institute for Southern Studies found that white county commissioners were overrepresented in proportion to white people's presence in the population. Although the disparity was not huge—77 percent of officials versus 66 percent of the population—over half of the state's counties had no African American representation at all. If descriptive representation matters, and evidence suggests it does, then local governments need to do a better job of ensuring that there are plenty of opportunities for blacks and other minorities to win office.

Finally, some advocates conclude that local governments and citizens should do their best to adopt an **equity lens**, or a framework that evaluates government policies and individual actions by their effects on promoting equality. Rather than some kind of specific effort or program, these advocates argue, racial equity needs to be a routine goal of government. Many of the solutions presented in this book, such as regional cooperation and more affordable housing, may gain even more support when adopting such an approach. A focus on equity and fairness should lead to better outcomes for everyone in local communities.

There are no easy solutions here. But the long history of racial discrimination in our local politics demands our ongoing engagement. And like the reformers of the civil rights movement of the past, we can continue to turn the story of diversity and equity in local governance from one of tragedy into one of triumph.

SUMMARY

- <u>Racial divides</u>, particularly due to the history of failed <u>urban renewal</u> projects, continue to have <u>significant and lasting effects</u> on local government and politics.
- The <u>civil rights movement</u> focused just as much on <u>reforming local governments</u> as it did on protecting rights on a national level.
- Although African Americans and other minorities have achieved dramatic gains in <u>representation and equality</u>, local governments and their citizens need to continue efforts to further reduce discrimination.

ACTION STEPS

- *Acknowledge the history and still-significant effects of racial divides on local government and politics.*
- *Support community empowerment efforts and organizations, including community-based development, services, and organizing.*
- *Support the recruitment and selection of people of color to elected and appointed office.*
- *Encourage your local government to adopt an equity lens in policymaking and action.*

WANT TO KNOW MORE?

There is an immense literature on urban renewal, housing discrimination, and racial divides in the post-war decades. I recommended some sources on the history of urban renewal at the end of the public transportation chapter; Jon Teaford's 2000 article "Urban Renewal and Its Aftermath" also provides a decent overview, although he is focused more on specific federal programs. Lawrence Vale has written many books on public housing in general that are worth reading, though the one most relevant to this chapter is probably 2013's *Purging the Poorest*. Kevin Kruse's 2005 book *White Flight* focuses on urban Atlanta, but also places white flight in the context of segregation and conservatism. Finally, Richard Rothstein's *The Color of Law* from 2018 is an award-winning primer on the widespread practice of redlining and its devastating effects on black wealth.

Two other resources of note on urban renewal: the Digital Scholarship Lab at the University of Richmond has an excellent online mapping tool (https://dsl.richmond.edu/panorama/renewal) that charts the families that were displaced by urban renewal; and if you are curious about how urban renewal was actually pitched in the early post-war years, University of South Florida's library has an online exhibit (http://exhibits.lib.usf.edu/exhibits/show/civil-rights-in-tampa/urban-renewal/) that includes the City of Tampa's Comprehensive Plan for 1956–1957, which, as the library's accompanying description notes, "laid the groundwork for the destruction of several Tampa neighborhoods."

A general explanation of descriptive representation can be found in Hanna Pitkin's 1967 classic *The Concept of Representation*; the case for its effectiveness in serving minority needs was offered most famously in a well-cited 1999 article by Harvard political scientist Jane Mansbridge. You can find a thorough study of deracialization campaigns from around the time of Black Tuesday in a 1997 volume edited by political scientist Huey L. Perry.

Adopting an equity lens is one of the strategies advocated by the Local and Regional Government Alliance on Race & Equity (https://www.racialequityalliance.org/), which, supported in part by University of California Berkeley's Haas Institute, works to engage local governments in policy reform.

BIBLIOGRAPHY/FURTHER READING

Ammon, Francesca Russello. 2016. *Bulldozer: Demolition and Clearance of the Postwar Landscape*. New Haven, CT: Yale University Press.

Dreier, Peter. 1996. "Community Empowerment Strategies: The Limits and Potential of Community Organizing in Urban Neighborhoods." *Cityscape* 2 (2): 121–59.

Kruse, Kevin Michael. 2005. *White Flight: Atlanta and the Making of Modern Conservatism*. Princeton, NJ: Princeton University Press.

Mansbridge, Jane. 1999. "Should Blacks Represent Blacks and Women Represent Women? A Contingent 'Yes.'" *The Journal of Politics* 61 (3): 628–57. https://doi.org/10.2307/2647821.

Orey, Byron D., and Boris E. Ricks. 2011. "A Systematic Analysis of the Deracialization Concept." In *The Expanding Boundaries of Black Politics*, 11:325–34. Series: National Political Science Review. Abingdon, UK: Routledge/Transaction Publishers.

Perry, Huey L., ed. 1997. *Race, Politics, and Governance in the United States*. Gainesville: University Press of Florida.

Pitkin, Hanna F. 1967. *The Concept of Representation*. Berkeley: University of California Press.

Rothstein, Richard. 2018. *The Color of Law: A Forgotten History of How Our Government Segregated America*. New York: Liveright.

Teaford, Jon C. 2000. "Urban Renewal and Its Aftermath." *Housing Policy Debate* 11 (2): 443–65. https://doi.org/10.1080/10511482.2000.9521373.

Vale, Lawrence J. 2013. *Purging the Poorest: Public Housing and the Design Politics of Twice-Cleared Communities*. Chicago: University of Chicago Press.

Yee, Allie. 2016. "On North Carolina's County Commissioner Boards, Racial Diversity Is Lacking." *Facing South*. September 9. https://www.facingsouth.org/2016/09/north-carolinas-county-commissioner-boards-racial-diversity-lacking.

WHAT'S NEXT?

Let's review.

This book started out by telling you a little bit about local government and politics, then provided an overview of the types and structures of local government. Then we got to the good stuff: the "right answers" in local politics—the issues where it is pretty clear what we should do.

Before we finish up, let's take a look back at those previous chapters and gather all the action steps we've found so far in one place.

ACTION STEPS REVISITED

Introductory Chapters
- *Advocate for home rule in your state; in general, the more local control, the better.*
- *Find out which form (for example, "weak-mayor") your local government uses, and try to learn some of the lingo/vocabulary so you are better informed.*

- *Get to know your local decision-makers—legislators and administrators. (They may be people you already know.)*
- *Consider running for office—it may not take much to win!*

Right Answer 1: No Taxpayer Funding for Stadium/Arena Projects

- *Be skeptical of claims about economic impact.*
- *Reject public financing for stadium and arena projects.*

Right Answer 2: Keep Housing Affordable

- *Support reform of local housing authorities.*
- *Support local laws that increase stock of affordable housing, from development incentives to inclusive zoning to community land banks.*
- *Support housing solutions from nonprofits, especially land trusts and banks.*
- *Help promote the idea of housing for all as an important right and social/economic need.*

Right Answer 3: Support Public Transit

- *Support investment in public transit.*
- *Support transit plans and systems that balance more frequency (to attract middle-class commuters) and coverage (to ensure equal access to the system).*

Right Answer 4: Say "Yes" to Regional Cooperation

- *Support efforts to build regional cooperation.*
- *Avoid major giveaways to lure in specific businesses/industries.*
- *Support development of broad infrastructure.*

Right Answer 5: Do NOT Cut Spending (Too Much)

- *Avoid candidates and officials who argue for slashing spending and cutting services, or who demonize bureaucrats as lazy and wasteful.*

- *Support reasonable and relatively efficient public spending on necessary services like parks, roads, libraries, and social services.*
- *Support initiatives to provide more efficient services such as e-government, performance budgets, and careful auditing.*

Right Answer 6: Support Racial Diversity and Equity

- *Acknowledge the history and still-significant effects of racial divides on local government and politics.*
- *Support community empowerment efforts and organizations, including community-based development, services, and organizing.*
- *Support the recruitment and selection of people of color to elected and appointed office.*
- *Encourage your local government to adopt an equity lens in policymaking and action.*

WHAT ELSE?

Beside all of these specific directives from previous chapters, there are just a few more things that you can and should do. In fact, there are three:

- Vote!
- Join a local civic association!
- Go to a public meeting!

All of these actions take time and effort, but not as much as you may think. I will explain the reasons for each in detail below.

Remember to Vote

As a politics teacher, I am almost contractually obligated to tell you to vote. But the idea that "one vote can make a difference" really has its most honest application at the local level. Elections for your local school board, county commission, or town tax collector are often tiny affairs, with very little media coverage, public understanding, or voter turnout. Local candidates depend heavily on each and every voter they win to their cause. This dependence has more than one consequence in terms of your own power.

First of all, you can make your voice heard on local issues. Do you think teacher pay is too low? Would you like to see a bus stop on your block? Do you wish someone in the city could do something about all those potholes? You do not necessarily have to be a policy expert; just tell candidates about the issues that matter to you and your neighbors. They should be listening if they want your vote, and they may desperately *need* your vote. This kind of logic becomes even more apparent if you have the interest and resources to take on other roles as well. If you write a check, put up a yard sign, or even host a house party or knock on doors, these things can only enhance your ability to bring government attention to an issue if and when your candidate takes office.

Of course, local elections bring a couple of challenges as well as opportunities. Most local contests are nonpartisan, at least on the surface, in a well-meaning effort to keep national-style ideological politics out. That is fine as far as it goes; the old saying that "there is nothing partisan about a pothole" holds a certain logic. But this also means that voters lack the "cues" that partisan labels often provide in national elections. I may not know who Homer T. Barnswallow is, but if I see he is a Republican, I have at least *some* idea of how he will perform as a city council member. Without those obvious cues, it is a lot harder for regular citizens to stay informed.

And information is harder to come by because, as I mentioned earlier in the book, local news sources are drying up. According to the Associated Press, over 1,400 towns and cities have lost their local newspaper since the year 2000; in addition, local television has become more oriented toward state and national news as local stations were and are being consolidated into corporate behemoths.

If you live in a major city, you probably still have a newspaper or two, and in many areas, large and small, enterprising citizens operate blogs or Facebook pages to promote local information. Still, many counties and municipalities have no local coverage at all.

One key bit of information that you absolutely have to know in order to vote is *when* to vote. You cannot avoid a presidential election even if you wanted to: the ubiquity of political ads and info about that particular contest makes it impossible to ignore, even in remote areas. But the local bond referendum or school board election could be in an odd year or in the spring. As with the lack of partisan labels, some localities have moved local elections away from the national cycle in order to keep nonlocal politics far away. But this means that you have to try to keep track of election dates. In Missouri, for example, all municipal elections are held on the first Tuesday after the first Monday in April (!?!). Even in St. Louis, Missouri's second largest city, turnout in the mayoral election of 2017 was only 30 percent. If you think that sounds ugly, turnout in the last election for St. Louis city council members without a mayor on the ballot was *only 10 percent*.

Based on those numbers, states like Missouri might be better off moving elections to a regular November cycle. But until they do, local voters need to stay on top of these odd schedules. You can get some help, thankfully: there are plenty of apps and websites like BallotReady, We Vote, and TurboVote that will track this information for you, as well as send reminders for registration deadlines and election days. If you get out and vote in even one of these off-schedule local elections, that may be enough to get you in the habit for similarly weird dates in the future.

Finally, voting is the most basic act of political participation, and the widespread use of the right to vote is a bedrock principle of democracy. But it is also an important political action step that you can use to "level up"—it starts you down the path of gathering information, evaluating public officials, and eventually, demanding accountability from your government through political organizing and action. When you vote, you are much more likely to stay informed, active, and engaged in local politics. It is a crucial first step.

Join a Neighborhood Group

Skeptics often warn that one vote cannot make a difference. Again, the vote margin in local elections can be quite small! But even if the "one vote doesn't matter" crew is right, a *group* of votes definitely makes a difference, at least in the minds of local candidates and officials. Local politics does not rely on interest groups as much as at the national level, but combined interests are just as significant in local politics in that local politicians have limited time and resources, and are more likely to listen to you if you join with other like-minded folks.

So whom and what should you join? Well, follow your interests and conscience, but one great option is a **neighborhood civic association**. Such associations can range from informal, irregular meetings to more formal nonprofit groups that together form what may be the most important shared interest in local politics—geography. If local politics is all about land use—I may have mentioned this once or twice above—then you and your physical neighbors share an important interest based on your location on that land. Civic associations discuss varied issues of concern to a neighborhood. You could be worried about crime, and are considering developing a Neighborhood Watch; you could be interested in helping local merchants to maintain the nearby strip mall; or you could be trying to rein in a troublesome business, like a manufacturing facility with too much truck traffic in the neighborhood.

Although civic groups are typically not political, they can be places where local public officials come to share information and hear about constituent concerns. Because their time and resources are limited, smart public officials would rather go to a place where they know they will find twenty active constituents than try to hear from them one at a time. This logic works for bureaucrats as well: a local planning commissioner or police lieutenant may find their job gets a lot easier if they have regular communication with citizens who might otherwise complain about their action or inaction on particular issues. These officials may even live within a civic association's borders; again, these folks are often people in your neighborhood.

For these purposes, even a private **homeowners' association (HOA)** meeting can work. Increasingly popular in suburban areas, HOAs are problematic, government-ish bodies, since they are often charged with enforcing "covenant" agreements on members. Basically, if you buy a home in an HOA-bounded community, you agree to pay fees to the HOA and abide by its rules. The upside of such an agreement is your ability to enjoy amenities run by the HOA like a pool, a clubhouse, or tennis courts; the downside is that you are limited in what you can do to your property. HOAs have earned a bad reputation, sometimes justified, as nothing but a bunch of snobs who dictate what color your house can be painted or whether you can put a playhouse in your backyard.

Still, whether or not this critique is fair, HOA meetings present a gathering sizeable enough to interest a local county supervisor or council member, a police officer, or a public works administrator. Even the snobbiest of HOAs is still a group of constituents, and meeting with it presents a chance to address concerns or even win votes for the next election. Particular HOAs may have specific rules preventing political activity, depending on the state and locality. Still, in most cases, there is no reason why residents cannot leverage regular HOA meetings to at least get informed by local government officials.

What if you live in an area without an HOA or civic association? Well, you can start one. It may be easier than it sounds. Citizens often band together informally in times of crisis, when

they perceive a threat to the community. Neighbors might gather
in a resident's living room, or the local church or rec center during
a crime wave or when a development seems to threaten the char-
acter of the neighborhood. But you do not have to wait for a
problem. If you just get some like-minded residents together—in
your home, or some kind of public meeting place like your local
library—you can see if there is an appetite for more. Once you
develop a core group that has interest and even a little time, you
can look into identifying more formal structures and leadership,
raising money, and maybe even forming a nonprofit organization.

At this point, it is important to note that this model of neighborhood group meetings may seem like a better match for wealthier
folks, particularly middle- and upper-class families with resources
like free time, and maybe even a nonworking parent. Wealthy
neighborhoods are often chock-full of overqualified stay-at-home
parents who put that law degree to work running the local fund-
raiser or cleanup effort. The idea of organizing a neighborhood
meeting may seem overwhelming to less affluent citizens, who
have enough trouble simply finding the energy to work multiple
jobs and put food on the table.

While some local governments and nonprofits offer useful
guides for starting an association, an even better step would be for
them to offer actual resources and funding. A great project for a
group like the United Way or other capacity-building nonprofits
would be to offer training, funding, and staffing support for
launching neighborhood associations in low-income areas. Such
a program could identify possible leaders, offer and/or book
meeting spaces, and especially provide food and childcare; these
efforts would go a long way toward lowering barriers to participation for lower-income citizens.

If you do have the resources, and whether or not you have
the option to join a civic group, your local government may have
other, more formal structures that can help you voice concerns

and participate in local politics. If you care about your local public schools—and you should, as they are important institutions supported by your tax dollars—then you can join your local **parent–teacher association**. If your local school does not have a PTA, again, you can start one. In most cases, you do not even need to be a parent of a child at the school; PTAs typically are open to all school district residents.

Many cities and counties also have **advisory boards** and **commissions** that oversee a host of legal, policy, and community concerns, ranging from parks to public health to historic preservation. Some are mandated by state or federal law: most cities and counties in Virginia have a "Community Criminal Justice Board," for example. Others are specific to a particular locality: Ohio's Cuyahoga County has a board of trustees just for the Soldiers' and Sailors' Monument, a commemorative statue in downtown Cleveland. But all of them may provide you with an opportunity to participate. Do you care about your local public library system? Join the citizen board that advises it. Do you have some interest or expertise in visual arts or healthcare? Apply to be appointed to the public commission that advises the city on your pet issue. To take just one example essentially at random: Sioux Falls, North Dakota, a city of fewer than 200,000 residents, has *over forty* of these organizations, many with regular vacancies.

These kinds of boards and commissions are often a mixed bag. Many of them mostly rubber-stamp the actions of public officials, or defer to bureaucratic experts who have the most knowledge about what is happening in the particular area covered. But if you are interested in a specific policy like homelessness or land development, these boards can be a good way to find out what is going on in your locality, as well as to meet the players involved. They can certainly lay the groundwork for meaningful work elsewhere. And who knows? Sometimes a particular board will have something worthwhile to do, or at least will provide useful input to policymakers.

One place where input certainly *does* matter from the jump: **zoning boards**. If (again) local politics is all about land use, then zoning boards are where the action is. County and city councils are often guided in development decisions by these boards. They may help set general zoning laws and regulations, and grant exemptions to these regulations for specific projects; they also may work with planning officials to approve development deals. Zoning boards are very often dominated by developers and their allies. Citizens may be well served by these experts, but it would help ensure fairness and that community concerns are addressed to have "regular" people join them as well.

Finally, if you have time after all of these groups and meetings, you may want to give other local civic organizations a try. Membership in traditional fraternal organizations like the Rotary, Elks, Lions, and Freemasons has been declining for decades, but is still strong in some areas of the country. Although these organizations have their problems, including reinforcing traditional hierarchies—the Rotary Club in Birmingham, Alabama, voted to stay whites-only as late as in *1982*—such civic groups have long been known to help build networks of civic participation. Social scientists, most famously Robert Putnam in the 2000 book *Bowling Alone*, have argued that the erosion of participation in these groups has contributed to the undermining of our "social capital," the networks of trust and engagement that support a healthy democracy. Joining up helps you connect with your neighbors, which is good for you—and good for our politics.

Of course, you may feel like your life is much too busy to devote any time to these groups. Chances are you *are* busy, but so is everyone. If you found enough time and money to read this book, I bet you can find an hour or two a month to join a board, PTA, or civic group. And if you do not currently have the means to do this, your local community should provide the infrastructure so that you can.

Attend a Public Meeting

Almost every city council, town board, or county commission meets at least monthly, if not more often, and their meetings are, by law, open to the public.

You should go.

It may not sound super-duper exciting to watch a bunch of public officials drone on about ordinances, haggle over budget numbers, and offer proclamations in favor of local Girl Scout troops. This is especially true in a modern era in which your other options are binge-watching Netflix, scrolling through your Instagram feed, or playing video games, plus all the other real-world things that sound so much more fun, like washing your hair or cleaning your kitchen. I get it: meetings are boring.

But these official meetings offer a chance to see how government actually *works*; you can see the players involved, get a sense of who they are and how they operate, and learn the language they use. (In Richmond, Virginia, for example, the city council often calls a law or ordinance a "paper," for some reason.) But not only do you get more informed about local politics, you learn more about specific policies. During these official meetings, local ordinances become local law. Issues with two sides may be tipped toward one of those sides. Your taxes, your neighborhood, your schools, your city or county could be affected in ways that are significant and long-lasting. If you are not present, you may not know about it; and if you are not present, you *definitely* cannot affect the outcome.

Showing up gives you a chance to make your voice heard. Most government meetings allow specific periods for public comment; you may not even have to sign up ahead of time. (Your local government body hopefully makes its rules clear.) No matter what, public speaking periods offer a chance to speak directly to those in power, sometimes right before they make an important decision. Plus, if there is an issue you support or oppose, you can bring friends; a council chamber filled with opponents to an ordinance will at least get council members to think twice before passing it.

As with civic groups, however, there is a class bias built into this call for attendance: you cannot devote time to politics if you are too busy making ends meet. So local governments should be doing everything they can to make it easier for people to participate. For example, the city of Alexandria, Virginia, implemented an initiative in 2012 called "What's Next Alexandria"—this was an ambitious citywide effort to develop new guidelines for civic engagement. The resulting *Handbook for Civic Engagement* offers a broad framework for actively engaging citizens in public projects. Importantly, the handbook also reminds city leaders to think about accessibility, including the availability of translation and childcare services, for public meetings.

In fact, *all* cities and counties should think long and hard about their schedule of public gatherings. Are meeting times feasible for working people to attend? Are meetings located near public transportation, and is free parking offered? Are there childcare services available for those who cannot find other options for their children? Are meetings recorded and/or streamed online, in the form of either audio or video, so that people who cannot attend can still see what is happening?

Making sure citizens can attend is only the first step; local governments also need to ensure that there are sufficient opportunities for these folks to provide substantive input on decision-making as well. One famous model of how to do this is Sherry Arnstein's "Ladder of Citizen Participation." In an influential 1969 journal article, Arnstein, a policy analyst and former federal bureaucrat, laid out how governments often set up meetings and processes that prevent true participation from "have-nots." Arnstein proposed a "ladder" of participation as a metaphor for better engagement— the further up the ladder that localities progress, the more citizen input and power can be found.

Arnstein's Ladder of Citizen Participation

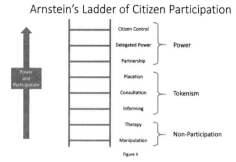

Figure 4

At the bottom level of her ladder (see Figure 4), governments mostly engage in what amounts to public relations, trying to win citizens' support without bothering to get their input or even actively rejecting input. The middle rungs allow for various levels of what Arnstein termed "tokenism": government officials may consult or placate citizens but still do not really want to listen to them. It is only at the top levels of the ladder—only with partnership, delegated power, or even full "citizen control"—that people are really engaged in decision-making. Of course, citizen control does not mean that elected officials should give up all authority and responsibility. They were elected to do a job and should not try to outsource basic functions to the public. But there are ways to engage citizens and gather input on development projects, locality-wide priorities and goals, and strategic planning—input that can inform day-to-day lawmaking.

Some more dramatic policy processes go even further. New York City, for example, is engaged in a "participatory budgeting" venture that allocates a certain amount of funding to city council members for capital projects; these projects are then voted on by constituents, with the top vote-getters receiving the money. Similarly, Greensboro, North Carolina, has a Participatory Budgeting Commission that helps collect and vet ideas, as well as funnel them to the city council; these proposals are eligible for a half-million dollars in funding. According to the nonprofit Participatory

Budgeting Project, over $300 million has been allocated through similar processes in dozens of localities across North America.

No matter what level of civic engagement is allowed by your local government, attendance at a public meeting is probably the starting point. If it is just not possible for you to attend in person, there are some other options. First, you can try to follow a livestream online or possibly on a local-access television channel. Some local journalists—or where local media is sparse or gone, local activists—have taken to live-tweeting or blogging about public meetings, so you can catch up there. Outside of the meetings, local governments are often subject to rules that make sure they solicit public input on policymaking, including gathering comments online and through email. These kinds of comments are not as influential as in-person statements at a live meeting, but they do represent actual constituent input that may be useful. Public officials may be as uninformed as anyone on particular issues, and you can point out something they do not know, for example. No matter what, officials do respond to public pressure if you mobilize your community. If a mayor or county commissioner sees a hundred emails on one side of an issue and none on the other, the math alone can sway them to your side.

Finally, if there is an issue that you care about, you should consider how to be a good advocate for that issue. Careful and effective advocacy is a goal of public comments at an official council or board of supervisors meeting, for sure, but it can also apply to a visit to your local representative at their office, if they have one. Or you may just run into them at a county fair or local coffee shop. If you do, unless they are busy with family or personal matters—even public officials should expect some measure of privacy—or are bleeding profusely, they should be willing to hear what you have to say.

To be a successful advocate, you should always be polite, be brief about what your concerns are, and especially remember to have a clear "ask." What *exactly* do you want the official to do?

If the official is a council member, should they introduce a new ordinance or vote for/against a pending ordinance? If they are an administrator—a county clerk, or the head of a city department—should they change the way they enforce a law?

In my classes, I often teach students a quick model for advocacy: the **EPIC model**, adopted from RESULTS, a national anti-poverty advocacy group. EPIC, based on its acronym, has four components:

- **Engage** your listener: get your listener's attention with a dramatic fact, short statement, or question. Keep this opening statement to one sentence if possible.
- State the **problem**: explain the problem you just introduced. What are the causes? How widespread or serious is it?
- **Inform** about solutions: tell the listener about a solution to the problem you just presented. Provide examples of how and where it has worked. Cite a recent study or tell a first-person account of how the solution has impacted you or others you know.
- **Call** to action: what do you want the listener to do? Make the action something specific so that you will be able to follow up. If possible, offer a simple yes-or-no question.

This model is just one way to operate in terms of advocacy. But no matter what approach you take, a polite but clear conversation with a public official will enable you to make your voice heard. Remember that you have every right in a democracy to hold public officials accountable for their decisions and to provide input to ensure those decisions are the right ones. And because these are local officials we are talking about, they are probably in your community right now, ready to hear from you and your neighbors. Again, that is the great thing about local politics: **access** and **impact**. Both are waiting for you—go out there and get engaged!

FINAL ACTION STEPS

- *Vote in local elections.*
- *Join your local civic association.*
- *Look for other opportunities to participate like PTAs, boards and commissions, and civic groups. Support resources to develop more of these organizations in your community.*
- *Go to a public meeting.*
- *Encourage your local government to offer accessible meetings that provide real opportunities for citizen engagement.*

LOCAL POLITICS MATTERS.

BIBLIOGRAPHY/FURTHER READING

Arnstein, Sherry R. 1969. "A Ladder of Citizen Participation." *Journal of the American Institute of Planners* 35 (4): 216–24. https://doi.org/10.1080/01944366908977225.

Bauder, David, and David A. Lieb. 2019. "Decline in Readers, Ads Leads Hundreds of Newspapers to Fold." *Associated Press*. March 11. https://www.apnews.com/0c59cf4a09114238af55fe18e32bc454.

City of Alexandria. 2014. "What's Next Alexandria: Handbook for Civic Engagement." Alexandria, VA: City of Alexandria.

Putnam, Robert D. 2001. *Bowling Alone: The Collapse and Revival of American Community*. New York: Simon and Schuster.

RESULTS. 2013. "Speaking Powerfully: The EPIC Laser Talk." Washington, DC: RESULTS.

ABOUT THE AUTHOR

Richard J. Meagher, PhD is Associate Professor of Political Science and Director of Social Entrepreneurship at Randolph-Macon College in Ashland, VA, and holds an MA in Philosophy and PhD in Political Science from the City University of New York. He lives with his wife and two daughters in Richmond, VA. He discusses state and local politics in local media and on his RVA Politics blog at rvapol.com.

ABOUT THE PUBLISHER

Lantern Publishing & Media was founded in 2020 to follow and expand on the legacy of Lantern Books—a publishing company started in 1999 on the principles of living with a greater depth and commitment to the preservation of the natural world. Like its predecessor, Lantern Publishing & Media produces books on animal advocacy, veganism, religion, social justice, and psychology and family therapy. Lantern is dedicated to printing in the United States on recycled paper and saving resources in our day-to-day operations. Our titles are also available as e-books and audiobooks.

To catch up on Lantern's publishing program, visit us at www. lanternpm.org.

facebook.com/lanternpm
twitter.com/lanternpm
instagram.com/lanternpm